s are saying

"Absolutely fabulous! Easy to understand! Marketing is finally fun for me!"
Peggo Hodes, *The Pegassus Band, music for kids*

"Great book! I just ordered several copies for my high school marketing students!"
Donna Sloan, *Marketing teacher*

"I was so impressed by Mini-Marketing that I recommended it to all my workshop participants at a national real estate conference in Scottsdale. King has done an outstanding job of simplifying the complexities of marketing, making it easy to understand basic concepts and develop simple, effective marketing plans. King also practices what he preaches about customer service! I never expected the long and helpful set of recommendations he sent me (without charge!) in response to a unique marketing situation I faced with my business. Two thumbs up for Mini Marketing!"
Rich Linkemer, Owner/Director, American School of Real Estate

"Thank goodness this is different from all those other marketing books which present way too much information to the point that I always feel intimidated and immobilized. This one is fast reading, exciting, full of graphics and fun exercises; a real treasure-trove of excellent marketing insights, tips, and important items not to overlook. King built upon my limited marketing knowledge to the point where I now feel like I really know what I'm doing. Very uplifting! I highly recommend it for both new and veteran business owners."
Michelle Dunklee, Territory Manager & Marketing Representative, CM Hospital

"You turned my thinking around without me even knowing it! Now I see marketing opportunities *everywhere*! And now I know what to *do* with them!"
W. Cunningham

"Mini-Marketing offers both roots and wings to entrepreneurs. While never losing sight of his clients' dreams, Ron offers a world of simple and clear information that is essential to making those dreams come true. This wonderful book -- marketing his own dreams and practical wisdom -- is an exemplary model of Ron's gift of inspiration and instruction. Read it and be inspired by an entrepreneur who both dreams and makes them happen."
Alan Crew, Psychologist

"Before reading Mini-Marketing, my own marketing was like throwing darts at a board: sometimes I hit a bullseye and sometimes I missed the target altogether. This book makes sure I hit the target every time, and that everything I do fits nicely into a strategic plan. I have to admit that I was really shocked that one of the author's simple mini-plans worked so well. He suggested showing customers some gesture of special gratitude, so on a lark I brought one of them donuts and muffins. They have since switched all of their business over to me and have become my largest account! *Mini-Marketing* has a special place on my bookshelf, and I refer to it constantly!"
Andrew Weiss, President, Above Discount Companies, *"Where Savings and Service Connect"* 800-599-9646, www.abovediscount.com. *(Printer for RKA Publishing: The Common Sense Press)*

"Your book has arrived, and I'm already half way through it. It's clear, concise, and constructive! Thank you!"
Bob Greenwood, *Sun.Ergos, A Company of Theater & Dance*

Mini Marketing©

The New Common-Sense Low-Cost Approach for Selling Yourself, Your Products, and Your Services

Ron King

PELICAN PUBLISHING COMPANY
Gretna 2002

First edition, 1997
Second edition, 1998
Third edition, 1999
Fourth edition, 2000
Fifth edition, 2001
First Pelican edition, 2002

Printed in the United States of America

Published by Pelican Publishing Company, Inc.
1000 Burmaster Street, Gretna, Louisiana 70053

This book
is dedicated to
my wife, Gerri
without whom
my life would be empty,
to my son, Ethan
whose perceptiveness
and encouragement
help me keep
everything in perspective,
and to my parents,
whose wisdom and energy
have always given me the courage
to do anything I want.

Due to the wonderful feedback from readers all over the country, this publication is updated frequently. If you wish to submit ideas for additions, changes, content, graphics, or whathaveyou, please do so at any time. Feel free to use the form in the back of the book.

A note from the author

I need to address my use of plural pronouns after singular words, phrases, and clauses, e.g.: "Each individual needs to understand ***their*** *role in the process."*

Author Bolles in "What Color Is My Parachute" suggests that just as the pronoun "you" is now used as either singular or plural, so the pronouns "they," "their," and "them" were once used.

According to "The Handbook of Non-Sexist Writing" authors Mullen and Swift, the singular/plural usage of those three pronouns is now very much evident "on the street" and should return to the written word as well. Thanks for the suggestion, and it will herein.

This also, thank goodness, helps me avoid using awkward substitutes like "he/she," and "s/he," and "her/his."

On the fundamentals of marketing, science, and all other disciplines....

"Most of the fundamental ideas of science (substitute "marketing")
are essentially simple and may, as a rule,
be expressed in a language
comprehensible to everyone."
Albert Einstein

"If you cannot,
in the long run,
tell everyone what you have been doing,
then your doing has been worthless."
Erwin Schrodinger

Table of contents

What makes this book unique...

Welcome entrepreneurs, students, teachers, and professionals; we're going on a journey. Because your mind works in mysterious ways, so, too, does this book.

It's the only marketing book I've seen that will take you by the hand, and then, through a series of exercises, humorous discussions, and anecdotes, gently teach you how to use the common-sense knowledge you have about business (or about your own business, if you have one) to develop a simple, successful marketing plan that really works -- and gets a passing grade!

"This book helps you transform what you do know about life and about your business into a marketing plan that works just for you."

It's a pretty subtle journey.

It's pretty easy.

And best of all, it's fun!

But more importantly, the concept behind this book is startling. I've never seen it *anywhere* else, so just knowing what it is will give you a *tremendous* advantage over your competitors. Simply put, from a marketing standpoint, there are two parts to every business that *must* be marketed separately. There's the product or service, of course, but just as important are all the components of the *business* that make it function. Whether your waiting room is comfortable has nothing to do with your product/service, nor does the way your business card looks or the way you present yourself on the telephone. However, the way you market these components can make or break your business. This books helps you see the distinction clearly, and to then do something about it.

Marketing does not have to be complicated, and you don't have to know a lot of fancy terms to make it work. Terms like "positioning," or "market segments," or "psychographics," or "niche" I'm sure all have their place, but not in *your* business at this point in time. I make a concerted effort to avoid them because they're an attempt to make marketing as "scientific" as possible, and I'm sure people that use them sound like they ought to be paid good money for their advice.

But it's the kind of advice you don't need right now – or maybe ever.

Put it this way: if marketing *was* a science, the billions spent every year experimenting with whether particular ads, or marketing strategies, or public relations campaigns, or colors, or whether to use a man's or woman's voice-over, would certainly have (by now, anyway) delivered a foolproof combination that worked every time and made millions for everyone in business.

But it hasn't.

So – if marketing isn't a science, what is it? And if it's not complicated, why isn't it? Here's why: After decades of marketing studies, marketing surveys, marketing polls, marketing *whatever*, "recent findings" show that just a plain old, good, trusting relationship is usually all it takes to convince someone to buy your products or services.

The easy part about all this, is that in your lifetime, you've had lots of relationships — with family members, friends, classmates, colleagues, bank tellers, loan officers, neighbors, dentists, doctors, teachers, store owners, mailmen/women, UPS people, and many others, so you already *know* what works and what doesn't.

You *know* that you get along better with people when you're nice. You *know* that being pleasant is a better way to start off a conversation than being disagreeable. You *know* when to stand up for something and when to compromise. You *know* when you make a date for dinner that you have to find a place *both* of you want to go.

It's safe, therefore, to say that you have a pretty intimate understanding of *the* most important aspect of marketing – the relationship.

Now all you have to learn is how to apply that understanding to your business. This easy-to-use workbook is designed to do just that. It will help you transform what you do know about life and about your business into a relationship-building marketing plan that works just for you and the business you want to develop.

What comes next?

Once you begin **Part 1**, the orderliness disappears. I'll take you in this direction, then that one. Then back again so we can come at it a different way, all the while moving forward to where you'll feel comfortable with who you are and what you know, what your business is all about, and where you want to grow with it.

If you read everything and do most of the exercises, you'll have a good, common-sense understanding of what marketing's all about. In **Part 2**, different marketing plan formats are discussed, and you can fill in the blanks to try some of them out for *your* business idea. Then, in **Part 3**, you'll find over 125 Mini-Marketing plans from which you can pick and choose, plans for marketing the *business components* of your business that you can use right away with little or no investment.

Where Part 3 is set up to help you market your *business* (such as marketing by using your image, customer service techniques, office procedures, referral sources, and word-of-mouth advertising). **Part 4** is a very comprehensive outline for figuring out how to market your particular *product/service*. This outline will help you figure out whether what you're *thinking* about selling makes any sense.

Naturally, Parts 2, 3 and 4 are closely linked and in some cases, they overlap. But that's OK! In marketing, just like in life, everything is related to everything else. Something done here creates a ripple over there. What you're trying to do is make the ripples big enough so people notice.

Part 5 is "What to do next!"

The Intent of This Book

is to help you understand marketing concepts, recognize the marketing skills and resources you already have, and help you acquire the additional skills and simple tools that will help you think creatively about marketing your services and/or products *as well as* the components of your business that make it work.

Further, if I can help you understand the reason and gain the confidence for using the information you already have, it'll become so second nature to you that it will no longer seem a chore.

I encourage you to complete the easy exercises throughout the book which will accomplish several things at once:

1. You'll clear your mind of bad marketing thoughts and will organize good thoughts in ways that enhance your marketing efforts.

2. You'll be creating resources that will help you develop other aspects of your marketing efforts, including your mission statement, marketing materials, marketing strategies, and identification of potential customers.

3. You'll understand how *more* business is uncovered by focusing on details; and

4. You'll learn to recognize the difference between marketing your *business* and marketing your *product/service*.

Preparing for a marketing plan is like preparing for a trip. You gather information, sort through it, make decisions about it, decide on the route and schedule, then get in your car and go.

It's the same with a marketing plan. Gather information about your potential customers: who they are, where they are, what they want, what they need. Look at the ways you can help them meet their needs, satisfy their wants. Then sort through it all, decide what you're going to do, then do it.

Introduction

First, you need to understand that a marketing plan is one part of a **Business Plan**. If you look at the outline of a typical business plan (it's coming up), you'll see that a marketing plan can only be accurate and useful if you've done all the rest of the homework required by the business plan.

Suppose you have an idea to start a store. Are there enough people in the area to buy what you want to sell? Are they willing to pay what you need to charge to make a profit? Where will you get money to buy enough items to fill the store? Which items will your customers want to buy? How do you know what they'll buy? Will you be able to stay in business during vacation season and everyone's out of town? If you know nothing about bookkeeping, do you have an expert you can hire? Can you afford to hire them? How large does your store have to be? Do you have parking? And so on.

Your business plan looks at all these kinds of questions to help you make sure you've thought of all the details before you go out and spend any money.

Trust me. It's cheaper to figure all this out on paper before you actually spend money starting your business.

Even if you have a business already, coming up with a business plan is essential because it helps you set goals. For instance, how much money do you need to make this year to pay your expenses (rent, leasing, wages, cost of goods to sell,

Before you go on, please see the next page for a typical Business Plan outline.

(Excuse me. Sorry to interrupt. I just wanted to show you what a typical Business Plan outline looked like. Note the marketing segments.)

1. Executive Summary
   - A. Purpose of plan
   - **B. Market potential**
   - C. Competitive advantages
   - **D. Product features**
   - E. Product development milestones
   - F. Financial results

2. Company Description
   - A. Business
   - B. Major products
   - C. Key customers
   - D. Applications
   - E. Distinct competence

3. **Market Analysis**
   - **A. Market description**
   - **B. Competition**
   - **C. Reactions from customers**

4. Projects and Services
   - A. User benefits
   - B. Patents and copyrights
   - C. Follow-on products
   - D. New technologies
   - E. Milestones and risks
   - **F. Marketing plans and programs**
   - **G. Selling strategies**

5. Operations
   - A. Location, equipment and facilities requirements
   - B. Production advantages
   - C. Costs

6. Management and Ownership
   - A. Key management positions
   - B. Background of personnel
   - C. Board of Directors
   - D. Current ownership
   - E. Materials availability
   - F. Quality control

7. Organization and Personnel
   - A. Staffing levels by type
   - B. Organization chart

8. Funds Required and Their Uses
   - A. Amounts and timing
   - B. Use of funds
   - C. Debt/equity mix
   - D. Terms
   - E. Investor payout
   - F. Compensation

9. Financial Data

Once you complete the research for the business plan, I **guarantee** you'll have a complete understanding of your product/service.

If you have a service or product other people might want, how will they ever know unless you tell them? Suppose you tell only one person, but that person has no money, or just bought the service or product from someone else. Then what? Do you give up? Or tell someone else what you have.

Herein lies marketing's basic concept: "Marketing is anything you do that lets someone else know what you do." If you don't market, no one knows what you do or have. If people don't know, they can't buy, and if they can't buy, your business will either never get going or wither away for lack of new customers.

If you're convinced you need to market, then *do* it! No need to spend a lot of time or money. Just decide how much, make a plan of what to do, then just commit to doing it!

A plan helps you determine the direction you want your business to grow, how fast you want the growth, and what you'll do to get it. It's like planning a trip. If you want to drive somewhere for a vacation, you get a map, make a plan, then go. Same with marketing. If you want your business to grow in a certain direction, you do some research, make a plan, then grow.

You don't need a complicated marketing plan. But you *do* need one, so throughout this book, I give you lots of options for creating one.

If you want to get started **right now**, go to the Mini-Marketing© Plans chapter, pick one of them, and follow the directions. Voila! You've started marketing.

The book's beginning chapters are helpful for people who don't know what marketing is, or they're afraid to do it, or they don't understand how to do it or why it's important. If you're in this group, don't be embarrassed. Almost every one of my customers is right there with you. One of the first things they tell me is that they don't like talking about themselves, and that the thought of putting themselves "out there" is positively nauseating.

"The mind is a wonderful thing. It starts working the minute you're born & never stops until you get up to speak in public."
Roscoe Drummond

Why wouldn't it be? Top on the list of stress-producing situations, even above the fear of death (which ranks 7th!), is the fear of public speaking. Add to that the idea of publicly speaking about yourself, and it's no wonder people avoid marketing. Talking about someone else is no problem. Talking about oneself is a whole other story, and people will avoid it at all costs, even at the cost of their business.

Eventually, I'll add several new chapters* addressing the emotional component of the marketing issue. Success sabotage, the imposter syndrome, fear of failure, procrastination, shyness, anxiety, low self-esteem, fear of public exposure -- are all giving the reluctant marketer plenty of reasons to award marketing a low priority.

My feeling is that if you know the reasons *behind* the reasons why you're resisting, you can choose to do something about it or find other ways to compensate.

In direct contrast to all of this, of course, is the clear knowledge that marketing is one of the few keys to your business's survival. If the buying public doesn't know what you do or what you offer, they won't buy, and the only way they're going to know, is for you to tell them.

So you have to market.

I need to tell you that it's really OK to talk about yourself and what you do. However, based on your level of self-esteem or what your parents taught you about not bragging, you might not be able to.

Let me just offer a couple of insights. First of all, there are probably lots of people out there who *want* your service or your product. As a matter of fact, if you've done your research well, you *know* there are lots of people who want it. It might be precisely what they need to solve a problem, satisfy a need or want, or just do the trick for a number of reasons. But because they don't know you have it (you haven't *told* them because you haven't done any marketing), they obviously can't buy it because they don't know where to find it.

Second of all, people are *always* looking for options: ways to improve, change, learn new things, save money, make money.

Again, if you've done your homework, the service/product you've designed is good for someone, somewhere, and presumably for many people, manywhere (my new word!). If you're convinced this is the case, then I, for one, won't totally buy into your fear of marketing. Because if you truly *know* you have a product/service people need/want, then you'd be remiss not to *share* it with all the people who *want* it. And maybe you'll even be a little *excited* about sharing it. As Rick Crandall says in his book *Marketing Your Services*, "If you're truly proud of what you

* If you send in the form at the end of this book, I will keep you informed of updates.

do, you can market honestly and effectively."

Let's put it this way. If you just designed a new product/service (call it "X"), and someone came up to you and said "Jane, for years I've been searching for 'X'. If someone offered me 'X' right now, I'd buy it in a minute!," what would you do? Say nothing? Or would you find some way to tell that person you have "X?"

You'd probably "find some way" to tell them. And that's what's important. Most all my workshop participants and other customers share the stereotype image about marketing. They see someone hustling a product, pressuring for a sale, so when we talk about their *own* marketing, they just can't see themselves in that role.

And I don't blame them -- or you. You should know right off, that though those high pressure sales tactics are still in use, they're becoming less and less effective and are therefore being abandoned in favor of more humane, sensitive approaches to building lasting relationships.

What I'm about in this book is to convince you of the *need* to market for all the reasons I've just talked about, and then to help you find the *ways* to market that fit your style, personality, and level of self-esteem, and that essentially help you feel comfortable during the process.

Well, there you have it. The Yin and Yang of marketing: don't want to market; have to market. Can't stand it; have to do it. Proud of what I do; afraid to tell people. *Really* want to put it off; if I *do*, my business will die.

But don't despair. This book is here to help. It's written with the underlying premise that you're in business because you have something of value to offer.

But just because you have an extremely good service or product does not mean you're good at marketing. Not only do I understand that, but I give you **big kudos** for admitting it and seeking help.

"I don't have the money" and "I don't have the time" are two of the most common excuses for doing no marketing. But they are shortsighted and downright -- well -- not very smart.

If they even cross your mind, you clearly do not understand that no marketing means no one knows what you do, which means *no business.*

Marketing your*self* is like pulling teeth. Something else is always more important, gets in the way, or is just plain more exciting to do. I know! It's the same for everyone! It's a battle I constantly fight. But you still have to do it, and do it consistently, and the best way is to make an appointment with yourself on a regular basis (Thursdays, 2-6 PM). Then treat it like an appointment with a customer. If you get a call to meet someone during that period, you say "I have another appointment at *that* time. How about tomorrow at 2?" (Who has to know the appointment is with yourself?)

If you *need* to break this appointment, it should only be for an emergency. You just broke your finger. You have a final tomorrow. Your partner just got downsized. But then you need to reschedule for another time, not too far away — just like you would with anyone else.

Please don't think you can just hire someone else to do it for you. First of all, the going rate for many consultants today is between $75 and $200 an hour depending on where they're located. If you want help 1 day a week at the least, that's between $600 and $1600 every week, or $30,000 to $80,000 per year (give or take a little). Not many small businesses can handle that.

The second caution is that the consultant is *never* going to know your business as well as you, and any relationships they build with your clients will do you no good if you ever need to let the consultant go. No relationship with you = no trust = no business = starting all over again.

The concession you could easily (and justifiably) make, is to find one or two professionals to help you:

- get started, evaluate strategy, ideas, or set priorities, and keep you motivated and on track (the mentor);
- develop a framework for *all* your imaging efforts, and to then help design and execute exciting and impactful materials including a letterhead, business card, and brochure or flyer or other promotional materials.

Starting out right

If you're already in business, and continue to get new customers, somehow, somewhere, marketing is taking place. You may not know exactly what it is. You may not be consciously aware of how you're doing it. But you're doing it, in which case, you should take stock, because if you can find out what you're doing, and increase it just a little, you'll have the beginnings of a plan, and business will soon be growing again.

One last time: even if you don't feel like you want to go through the planning process, ***do something, and do it consistently***! Once you get going, and marketing becomes a routine part of your month/week/day, you will be amazed at the results.

Get Started Today!

An introductory note:

A New View
A New View
of your business

A dramatic turnaround in the way companies view customers has occurred during the past several years. Tremendous competition for limited dollars, and recognition that 70% of sales should be generated by existing or previous customers has forced customer-driven companies to spend considerable effort and dollars on maintaining their "customer base."

In the service industry as well, these same changes are forcing entrepreneurs and professionals to begin adopting terminology more befitting a business environment. Hence, as an example, "clients" or "patients" have become "customers." If you can think along these lines as well, it will give you a clearer view of the business of managing the buyers of your services and/or products.

We recommend that you begin thinking of and referring to these people as "customers" (at least internally) and that you work toward having a "customer-oriented service program." Customers look to buy both services and products, both of which you have the potential of offering. A truly customer-oriented service program is designed entirely around what benefits the customer, not what benefits your business, because the customer *is* your business. Without the customer making the decision to "buy," you *have* no business.

Is this a small point — referring to "customers" rather than "clients?"

Using the word "customer" will help you think differently about growing your business.

I don't think so. I think it will affect your mindset such that more creative ways to get — and keep — customers will result. You will also be forced to:

- learn the nuances of managing a customer base,
- keep current with new marketing ideas,
- feel comfortable with marketing lingo,
- get more in tune with your customers and what they *really* want from you, and
- create your own niche among your colleagues.

While they're merely selling to their clients, you're "responding to your customers' needs, wants and desires," and positioning yourself for more rapid growth and the ability to take advantage of marketing opportunities when they come along.

A Brief History of Marketing

The concepts behind "marketing" have been practiced for centuries. If marketing can be simply defined as letting someone else know what you do, then pounding on gourds and smoke signals were a form of marketing. If you want to see a movie with a friend, or go out for dinner, what you do to steer your friend to a movie or restaurant of your choice is marketing. Crying is a great way for a baby to market its needs. The sole function of a lobbyist is to market his/her clients' ideas. MCI markets its long distance service all the time. You market your ideas to volunteer committees, the school board, the newspaper editor. "Marketing" is everywhere, and you're always doing it regardless of what you think.

Marketing of the '50's and '60's adopted a term which is still used today. The idea behind "mass marketing" was to send out a massive amount of information in the hopes that someone would respond. Big billboards, magazine and newspaper ads, roadside Burma Shave signs, the Yellow Pages, and the door-to-door Fuller Brush salespeople were all forms of mass marketing. Because in those days companies had few competitors, and because buyers were largely uninformed, mass marketing worked quite well: enough people responded that companies were happy with the results.

Then changes started occurring. More competition, a larger population, more sophisticated buyers, more options for "advertising," women going to work outside the home -- all led to confusion about how best to reach people, and a riskier outcome for "mass marketing" techniques and dollars spent.

So in the mid'60's, marketing concepts began to change, as well. The idea was to try sending "buy me" messages only to the people who displayed a higher probability of responding. Crude surveys began providing basic information about buying habits, and vendors of both products and services started singling out specific groups as "targets" for their marketing campaign materials.

Trying to keep track of which targets got which messages was almost impossible before computer technology, but someone put it to use sorting datapunch cards which led to the sophisticated databased programs in use today. Databases allowed the gathering and storage of vast quantities of data that could then be sorted and used in creative ways. Keeping track of buyers, for instance. What they bought, when they bought it, and how much they spent, began providing insight about buying habits which was used to design marketing campaigns to get more business.

Databased marketing is still very much in use today. The cards grocery chains force you to use at the checkout keep track of who you are and what and how much you buy. Radio Shack always keeps track of these details. Readers Digest advertisers put one version of an ad in the eastern addition, another in the western, and then track responses to determine which ad is more targeted and gets more response.

Everyone is on to databased marketing. Service and product vendors send out mailings targeted to specific individuals (Dear Randy...). And buyers are becoming more wary as their mailboxes get bombarded every day with "targeted," but junk mail, that they throw away without reading.

Marketers have begun to realize that without a personal relationship with customers -- one that involves trust and caring -- customers aren't as likely to respond. Marketers have determined that the "relationship" is an important part of the sell-buy transaction, so "relationship marketing" is the newest strategy designed to use databased information to help develop individual connections.

The relationship may be a by-product of a series of satisfactory transactions. Or it may be an outright attempt to establish and maintain face-to-face contact with a customer. Focusing on the relationship almost always results in a better understanding of the customer's needs. And when a customer's needs are understood, better value can be delivered — which further results in increased customer loyalty and increased profits.

The customer is a highly valued individual with unique needs. If designed right, relationship marketing recognizes and addresses those needs for each of the individuals on the vendor's database.

What makes a relationship important in the buying process?

If you've bought a house, car, a meal in a restaurant, some clothes, shoes, or similar items recently — or changed physicians or dentists or auto parts stores, think about the process you went through in reaching a decision to buy the product or service.

How did the way in which you interacted with the vendor (the salesperson, the doctor, the mechanic) affect your decision to buy? I'll bet that the more friendly and caring the interaction, the more satisfied you were with it.

In your own business, then, figuring out exactly what makes the "vendor-customer" relationship work -- in the beginning and over the long term -- will give you the edge you need to grow.

A Quick Primer on Marketing

If you own a business, there are two parts of it that have to be marketed.

1. The business itself, which includes whatever it takes to keep it running and selling.
2. The services/products you're selling.

Few people understand this distinction and lump everything together. The result? Many important factors are overlooked.

Here's a quick perspective:

Why bother marketing? Because without it, no one knows who you are or what you have to offer.

What's the concept behind marketing? Creating an image that has value.

Before the public buys *anything*, they need to perceive a product or service as having value. If they know nothing about it, or if they see it or hear about it but don't understand it or can't relate to it, they won't buy it, regardless of how much potential it has to solve one of their problems or fulfill one of their needs.

So it's not the product or service they actually buy. It's the image of it they hold in their minds. If that image has value in that it fits within their perceived set of wants or needs, they'll buy that image. That image is represented by the actual service or product.

Keep in mind: You should never try selling the actual product or service. You should only sell what it does for the customer, because that's all the customer really wants to know.

What's the goal of marketing? Making the right customers aware of the benefits of your services/products.

What's the definition of marketing? Doing anything that lets the right people know what benefits you offer.

What needs to be marketed?

1. Your business.
2. The benefits of your services/products.

Part 1

Marketing Your Business

What is Marketing?

It's important that you develop a working definition of marketing so you know what you're going after and what you're trying to achieve.

The definition needs to be one with which you are very comfortable. It needs to trigger thoughts that are yours and that inspire you: when you're feeling lost about your business, when you wonder why you're spending time "marketing" when nothing you do seems to be working, or why you're spending marketing dollars with no proof that your investment is really paying off.

In my workshops, I always ask people to tell the rest of the group what they think marketing is. Here's how they answer the question: "How would you define marketing?"

Marketing is:

- letting people know; if they know, they'll come.
- friendly persuasion.
- schmoozing.
- a systematic way of presenting your business to the public.
- commitment.
- a way of convincing yourself that you have something to offer.
- a way of valuing yourself; believing you have a right to offer something.
- a way to move beyond word of mouth.
- exposure.
- a way to present how your service/product is essential to the community.
- convincing people I'm unique.
- inspiring confidence.
- creating and disseminating an image that portrays what I have to offer to paying customers.
- Anything I do to ensure a stable and increasing customer base.
- Getting info out to people who are really looking for what I have to offer.

So--

How would **you** define marketing?

Some ideas to get you started:

- What does marketing do?
- When should marketing be used?
- What's the purpose behind marketing?
- Who should market?
- What should marketing accomplish?
- Do you use some other term you like better?

(see next page for some other ideas)

Here are some simple definitions.

If they help, use them!

"Marketing
is anything you do
that lets someone else
know the benefits of what you do."
(Ron King)

"Marketing
is anything you do
that just might
create business for you."
(Ron King)

"Marketing
is anything you do
that helps a potential buyer
become aware of the benefits
of your service or product."
(Ron King)

"Marketing
is anything you
do to get or keep
a customer."
(Michael Porter)

"Marketing is the process of planning and executing the conception, pricing, promotion, and distribution of ideas,goods, and services to create exchanges that satisfy individual and organizational goals."
(American Marketing Association)

16 Good Reasons
why you shouldn't bother marketing

Do you agree?
Check here!

- ◯ • Someone else will do it for you.
- ◯ • If you're good enough, they'll find you anyway.
- ◯ • You hate to brag about yourself.
- ◯ • You're too self-conscious.
- ◯ • You really don't want public recognition.
- ◯ • Someone will find out you're not really that good anyway (the Imposter Syndrome).
- ◯ • You don't have the money.
- ◯ • You don't have the time.
- ◯ • You hate being rejected.
- ◯ • It's against your profession's protocol, ethical standards, etc.
- ◯ • If you keep yourself hidden, no one can point a finger if things go wrong.
- ◯ • You have a fear of networking.
- ◯ • You can't stand feeling like a salesperson.
- ◯ • You don't have any idea how to anticipate your customer's needs.
- ◯ • You don't explain things well.
- ◯ • Your target group keeps changing, and you don't want to keep starting over.

All right. Let's have them. Give me all the other reasons why *you* don't want to market.

◯ ____________________

◯ ____________________

◯ ____________________

◯ ____________________

◯ ____________________

◯ ____________________

◯ ____________________

◯ ____________________

◯ ____________________

Figure it out!

The more clear you are about your reasons for not marketing, the easier it will be to deal with them. An example: "You're harboring a distrust of salespeople based on a personal experience 15 years ago. You equate selling with marketing and don't want even a remote link to either of them."

Once you figure this out, you can put it into perspective. Then you can go about designing important parts of your marketing plan so they don't look like sales packages and don't require you to represent yourself as a salesperson. For instance, if you can accurately identify the dislikable characteristics and tactics of the salesperson(s) you remember, you'll probably automatically do the exact opposite. If dishonesty was one of those characteristics, no doubt you'll do everything in your power to be honest and provide the most reputable services and products available.

So again, go back and figure out exactly why you don't want to market. It's a good exercise. And if you come up with some really *great* reasons that aren't addressed in this book one way or another, *please* let me know.

29 better reasons
why you *should* market

- It will help you stay in business!
- You'll get more bang for the buck.
- You'll make more money.
- As customers move out of your region, you'll be able to adjust your plan.
- It'll help you avoid colluding with the power of denial.
- It will give you incentive and motivation.
- It will increase your customer base.
- You'll keep your name foremost in your customers' minds, and keep them away from your competition.
- You'll be able to focus the practice/business.
- You'll be able to identify targets of opportunity.
- You'll continually strengthen your image.
- It will help expand the impact of your word of mouth marketing.
- You'll be able to figure out what needs to go into your brochure/business card and other marketing materials.
- You'll be able to figure out the best way to establish credibility in your community.
- You'll have the opportunity to integrate your strengths and interests.
- It helps you become self-empowered and gives you a choice in a tough market.
- It provides a way to measure marketing successes.
- It'll give you a chance to look at what competitors and colleagues are doing.
- You'll develop your own set of marketing tools.
- You'll learn how to be effective reaching out to (schools, corporations, individuals).
- You'll get ideas for marketing alternative services in a conservative market.
- You'll learn how to pull people in and not drive them away.
- It'll help you figure out how to implement "differential marketing."
- You'll learn how to penetrate various systems and organizations.
- You'll create interest in yourself and in your products/services.
- It will help you establish/keep a good image.
- You'll be able to take advantage of networking opportunities.
- You'll move inventory.
- It will get you out of the office.

Elements and factors that are considered part of marketing

- products/services
- image/perception/packaging
- promotion/PR/advertising
- communication
- target group/prospective customer/ end user/public
- wants/desires/needs
- research (marketing is an intentional process)
- plan/strategy
- pricing/profitability
- positioning
- expectations/value
- delivery
- relationships
- relationships
- relationships
- relationships
- relationships

Marketing Objectives

- retaining existing customers
- leveraging contacts with, and expanding services to, existing customers
- attracting committed customers
- managing your image with existing and prospective customers
- generating controlled, profitable growth
- offering services designed to satisfy needs and expectations of customers and prospective customers

What is a Marketing Plan?

A Marketing Plan
is a formally prepared
document that identifies potential
clients and the critical
components of your business,
determines the best way
to market them
(the strategies),
and details exactly
what you're going to do
to make the strategies work.

Marketing Plan Development

Here's how to figure out whether you need a marketing plan.

1. **Assess your business**: Compare this year's income and expenses to last year's. What factors are contributing to the current status of your business?

2. **Make some predictions**: Given your existing state of affairs, how will you be doing a year from now? Are you OK with that? If you don't like what you see:

3. **Set new goals and objectives** that are reasonable

4. **Decide on one or two strategies** (based on what you *can* do, not what you'd *like* to do) to set these new goals in motion (e.g.: "I'd like to do 10% more business, or more networking, follow-up, public relations, repeat business, etc.").

5. **Decide on the tactics to implement those strategies**: What's the simplest way you can implement them with *consistency* within a budget that's 2-7% of your gross income, and which consumes no more than 20-40% of your time? What exactly will you do, and how will you do it?

6. **Evaluate and reassess your plan** after 3 or 6 months, make necessary changes, regroup, and keep going.

Why do you think *you* need a marketing plan?

	Reasons for developing a marketing plan
1	
2	
3	
4	
5	
6	
7	
8	
9	
10	
11	

* Some ideas: make more money, keep existing customers, get more customers, change course of businesss, be positioned for future, attract new colleagues, improve public image, enhance reputation

Take a look at your reasons and the implied expectations. Do you have a clear idea of exactly what you need to do to meet those expectations? If not, read on.

Ron's

Immutable ^marketing Laws

1. Only market to those people who can respond to it. Otherwise, it's an expensive, uphill battle.

2. The more clear you are about your services and products, the easier it is for people to appreciate them.

3. The more focused you are, the more opportunities you'll find.

4. You'll have better luck selling people what they *want*, not what you think they *need*.

5. The market is always driven by past, present, and future customers.

6. Market consistently, regardless of what or how much you do.

See the bibliography for *The 22 Immutable Laws of Marketing* by Ries and Trout.
And see the next page for another marketing gem!

The value of ^ ConSiStency

(another immutable marketing law)

One of the downfalls of any marketing program, regardless of its size -- actually probably the one factor singularly *most* responsible for the failure of any marketing activity -- is lack of consistency. In 1885, Thomas Smith wrote the following. Though it's about advertising, the lesson is clear. It takes people a **long time** to make decisions, especially if the decision is not an easy one, or if it involves something about which they may be unfamiliar.

Deciding to buy your product or service may be one such decision.

(Please excuse the gender bias. Smith obviously had no clue.)

1. The first time a man looks at an ad, he doesn't see it.
2. The second time, he doesn't notice it.
3. The third time, he is conscious of its existence.
4. The fourth time, he faintly remembers having seen it.
5. The fifth time, he reads the ad.
6. The sixth time, he turns up his nose at it.
7. The seventh time, he reads it through and says "Oh brother!"
8. The eighth time, he says, "Here's that confounded thing again!"
9. The ninth time, he wonders if it amounts to anything.
10. The tenth time, he will ask his neighbor if he has tried it.
11. The eleventh time, he wonders how the advertiser makes it pay.
12. The twelfth time, he thinks it must be a good thing.
13. The thirteenth time, he thinks it might be worth something.
14. The fourteenth time, he remembers that he wanted such a thing for a long time.
15. The fifteenth time, he is tantalized because he cannot afford to buy it.
16. The sixteenth time, he thinks he will buy it someday.
17. The seventeenth time, he makes a memorandum of it.
18. The eighteenth time, he swears at his poverty.
19. The nineteenth time, he counts his money carefully.
20. The twentieth time he sees the ad, he buys the article or instructs his wife to do so.

The Brand Called "You"

"Regardless of age, regardless of position, regardless of the business we happen to be in, all of us need to understand the importance of branding. We are CEO's of our own companies: Me, Inc. To be in business today, our most important job is to be head marketer for the brand called YOU.

"The good news -- and it is largely good news -- is that everyone has a chance to stand out. Everyone has a chance to learn, improve, and build up their skills. Everyone has a chance to be a brand worthy of remark."

Tom Peters, *Fast Company* Magazine, August: September 1997.

So what does it mean to market a brand? To build one up? And just what is a brand, anyway? More importantly, with all the other stuff going on with the business I'm trying to run, how can I take on something else like building up, managing, and marketing "Brand Me?"

What's important to understand, is how it all works together with what you're now doing.

A brand, according to Webster, is "a kind, grade, or make, as indicated by a stamp, trademark, or the like" (i.e.: the best "brand" of coffee). Unfortunately, the owner of a business can't just decide to "brand" a product or service, because a "brand" is also affected by perception. When customers have sufficient experience with, or exposure to, a product or service -- enough to form an image in their minds about it -- the brand *they* give it may end up being different from how *you* think it ought to be. And you may not like the brand *they* come up with!

There are other places in this book where I talk about image, but here's another aspect. One of the differences between YOU and Nike is money. If they don't like the way the public branded them, they just push more money into programs designed to change the public's minds.

You and I don't have that option, so we can't even *begin* thinking like that. What we *do* need is some way to manage the limited resources we *do* have so we can create our own image and hopefully get branded for the person (or business) we are -- or want to be.

This is where it gets a little tricky, because you've already been branded. When people think about you, they already have an image of you in their mind's eye, and unless you're new to an area, that image has been built over the years based on what you've done in the community, where you've volunteered, your work ethic, your family, etc., etc. As an example, when I say "elephant" to you, you picture an elephant, not a giraffe. And when you picture the elephant, there's a good chance you picture its strength, or have an image of it pushing over a tree, or pulling a heavy object. All of this makes up the image of an elephant which you carry with you.

The Elephant's Brand

The elephant could take this image and use it to develop a brand (call it "The Elephant Brand"), and based on your image of the elephant, you would assume that anything with "The Elephant Brand" label would be strong and be able to push or pull with some authority! In this case, "The Elephant Brand" is positive and persuasive.

Now what about *you*? What is the image people have about you and your business? And how have they used that image to "brand" you? "Ron King? He's that guy who knows all about small business marketing. Great Guy!" or "Jane Spear? Isn't she the one who helps you plan big events with no hassle?" or "Al Jolt? He's that weird guy who always gets the last word in. Some kind of a consultant, I think, but I've heard he's not very good."

If your "brand" is already positive and has the potential to help you in every aspect of your business, wonderful! Stick with it and build on it. If the public characterization of your brand is something you don't like, however, it'll be hard to change it. In that case, move out of town and start over, or be prepared to spend lots of time and dollars trying to change the public's image of you and your "brand."

Assessing Your Brand

As you properly surmise, managing every action and aspect of your life can be very complicated, and you could end up being paranoid about everything you do, which would be extremely restrictive.

But because every entrepreneur starts off on the same foot (already being branded by the public), the best thing is to get a sense of what that brand is and work with it.

What makes you stand out? What have you done this week to make yourself distinguishable from your competitors? If you polled your friends and customers, which of your personal traits would they say are most noteworthy? If you were to ask them what they thought were your strengths, what would they say? Can you comfortably build on both those characteristics? Do you like your customers? Do you like servicing them?

Keep in mind that, from this point on, everything you do in and outside your business will affect the brand called YOU. And because everything you do should be considered part of your marketing strategy, you are building and refining your "brand" every day.

What makes you Unique?

Here are some individual characteristics that might make you stand out from the crowd. You should **Add** to this list, **Determine** what applies to you and in what order of importance, then **figure out** how you can market that aspect of yourself and how you conduct your business. Later we'll have to look at what makes your product/service unique.

How would you explain to your potential customer that you possess some particular characteristic, or thought process, or training, or way of looking at the world, or way of recognizing the customer's needs, or particular combination of skills or talents that gives you a different perspective, or....?

I (or I'm):

❑ Cost-effective
❑ Confidential, discreet
❑ Customer-centered. Cooperative. I develop plans/ideas *with* you, not *for* you.
❑ Accessible
❑ Ethical
❑ Personal; Individualized
❑ Very astute
❑ Have a multi-problem approach
❑ Not caught up in red tape
❑ Giving, helpful, compassionate, understanding, a good listener
❑ Great at problem solving
❑ Have expertise and am well-trained
❑ Nurturing

❑ Believe in inherent goodness
❑ Quickly grasp environmental/historical context
❑ Non-judgmental
❑ Certified, well-regulated
❑ Experienced/have wisdom
❑ Continuously growing professionally
❑ Accountable
❑ Have diverse areas of expertise
❑ Innovative, creative
❑ Charitable - community oriented
❑ Enthusiastic, energetic, present
❑ Committed
❑ Nondiscriminatory
❑ Provide rapid relief
❑ Energetic/Dynamic
❑ Versatile
❑ Use humor/laughter

❑ What else?

* Use these characteristics in everything you do to create a great image about you and your business!

What REALLY makes you unique?

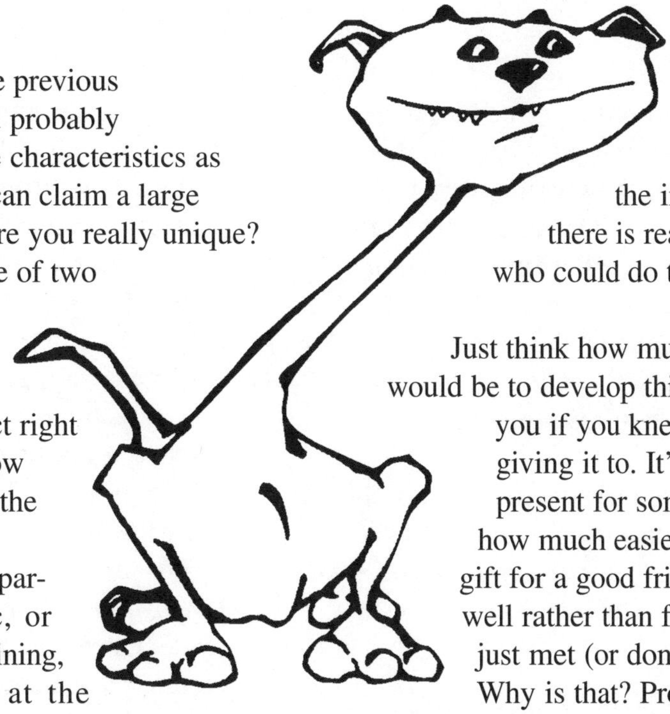

Take a look at the previous list. You could probably claim all these characteristics as yours. If you can, or can claim a large percentage of them, are you really unique? Suppose you were one of two people trying to get noticed by a potential customer and you felt you were the exact right person for the job. How would you explain to the customer that you possessed some particular characteristic, or thought process, or training, or way of looking at the world, or way of recognizing the customer's needs, or particular combination of skills or talents that gives you a different perspective, or....?

I know you may not be the only one in the world who could do the job, but you may be the only one in the *customer's* world to do the job exactly as they need to have it done, and that's what's important.

This is why it's critical to know exactly who your customer is. Later in this book, we'll focus on that as well, but here is the perfect place to start thinking about it.

You need to sort yourself out from the rest of the pack, to figure out what you have for talents, training, experience, outlook, approach, personality, body language, that come together in such a way that a potential customer will be absolutely smitten by you! Well, if not smitten, certainly very impressed. By the time you get done speaking with them, and/or showing them your materials, they should have the impression that there is really no one else who could do the job as well!

Just think how much easier it would be to develop this "package" of you if you knew who you were giving it to. It's like buying a present for someone. Think how much easier it is to buy a gift for a good friend you know well rather than for someone you just met (or don't even know). Why is that? Probably because with the friend, you feel comfortable because you know their tastes, hobbies, and what makes them smile. If you could just find out the same things about your potential customers...

Is that possible? Well, yes, it is. Maybe not to the same degree, but perhaps close enough for the business world. As you go through these pages, try thinking how you would find out this kind of information about potential customers who are relative strangers.

Matter of fact, why wait?

Let's do a short exercise here just to get you started. In a few pages, we're going to define exactly what service/ product you are offering to prospective customers.

When you developed your service/ product, you must have had someone (or some group) in mind. Who was it? How

What REALLY makes you unique?

(continued)

do you know (or did you find out) they needed it? Do they need it because they have a particular thing going on in their lives or businesses? Or because they won't be able to work as efficiently without it? Or because without it they're blocked from doing something they really need to do? Or because it's a better replacement for something they *need* to replace?

Once you can answer these kinds of questions, you have begun to identify something about your group of prospective customers. This group will become your "target" group.

What else about this group? Do they tend to fall in the same age or income brackets? How about their education? Should they be self-employed (for you to have a greater impact on them)? Should they have kids? Should they like to travel? Should they drive fast cars? Should religion play a big role in their lives? Do they want to make their businesses more successful?

In answering these "should" questions, you're beginning to define the kind of person/group for whom you designed your service/product. The more tightly you can draw this definition, the more exacting you can be about the prospective customer's tastes, hobbies, and what makes them smile. Once you do that, you have a match: your unique characteristics and the way you package them for sale, and their desire to buy (or at least seriously consider!) that uniqueness.

Let's tie this down right here by first getting you to define your ideal customer (who will eventually represent your "target" group). The clearer you are about this customer's specifics, the better you will understand how you can help them out.

Take a moment to figure out a very accurate profile of who you think your customer is. Keep in mind that your job is to narrow this down to the essence of your best and most ideal customer. When you get done, this profile should *not* fit anyone else's customer, and the profile should *clearly* demonstrate that only *you* with your special talents, training, product, offering, etc., etc., can help them out.

EXACTLY *WHO* is your customer?

How old is your customer? ______________________________

Where do they live? ______________________________

How far should they come to buy your product/service?? ______________________________

What kind of education should they have? ______________________________

Should they have children? ______________________________

Should they be married? ______________________________

What kind of income should they have? ______________________________

What kind of business should they be in? ______________________________

What position should they hold? ______________________________

What influence should they wield? ______________________________

In what timeframe should they be able to make a decision to purchase? ______________________________

What kind of training should they have? ______________________________

Do they need a fax, modem, or email to do business with you? ______________________________

If they work for a company, what size should the company be in annual revenues? Number of employees? ______________________________
____

What sorts of hobbies should they have? ______________________________

Should they have previous experience with a particular product/service? ______________________________

Should they be frustrated about something? ______________________________

Should they have already identified a need for your product/service? ______________________________

Do they need to be part of a referral network? ______________________________

Should they have been in business at least _____ years? ______________________________

____ ______________________________

____ ______________________________

____ ______________________________

Now...

Write this in a paragraph format, so it sounds good and clearly describes your ideal customer. If you think an entity (like a corporation) is your customer, forget the thought. No matter what you're selling, the "buy" is always made by a person, maybe even a group of persons, but definitely human beings, not organizations. And it's the quality of the relationship you have with those people that will make or break the sale.

So again, take this moment to write a clear and complete description of your ideal customer.

My ideal customer is:

What makes your product/service Unique?

Here are some individual characteristics that might make your ***products/services*** stand out from the crowd. You should

- Add to this list,
- Determine what applies to your products/services and in what order of importance,
- Then figure out how you can market those qualities. (For a thorough discussion and workplan on product/service development, please refer to Part 2 "Marketing Your Service/Product.")

❑ Less expensive than others	❑ ________	❑ ________
❑ More color choices	❑ ________	❑ ________
❑ Lighter/heavier	❑ ________	❑ ________
❑ More efficient	❑ ________	❑ ________
❑ Always on time	❑ ________	❑ ________
❑ Takes less time	❑ ________	❑ ________
❑ Uses proprietary formula	❑ ________	❑ ________
❑ Award-winning	❑ ________	❑ ________
❑ It's faster	❑ ________	❑ ________
❑ Makes jobs easier	❑ ________	❑ ________
❑ Helps you succeed by	❑ ________	❑ ________
❑ Combines tasks	❑ ________	❑ ________
❑ ________	❑ ________	❑ ________
❑ ________	❑ ________	❑ ________

"I have the premier, foremost, best, leading, superb business in the region for (less than 25 words):

____

____

____

____"

Let's go back
to something I said some time ago:
You should ***never*** *try selling*
a product or service
based on its features.
You should only sell
what it does for your customers,
because that's all
they really want to know.

And what benefits does your product/service give to your customer?

Identify the "features"
of your product/service,
then make an exhaustive list
of the **benefits**
of each of those features,
because the *benefits*
are what you'll market and sell,
not the features.
The more benefits you identify,
the easier the task of preparing
your marketing plan, because
you'll know exactly who
will be happiest getting them.

Figuring out the benefits is not easy...

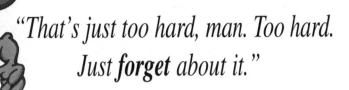

*"That's just too hard, man. Too hard. Just **forget** about it."*

I recently added this section, because I'm finding that many people are still not getting the concept about benefits.

People don't buy the actual product or service. Well, they *do*, but not just because it's what it is. Another words, you wouldn't buy a lawnmower unless it actually cut grass, would you? In this case, the name "lawn" and "mower" kind of suggests what it is this machine does, but suppose the product was a "Gizmat," and it was selling for 25 bucks. Last time you were in Wal-Mart, you saw a whole shelf of them.

Would you plunk down 25 bucks and buy one? I assume you wouldn't, at least not until you knew what it did, right? And that's exactly what I want you to think about. You're not going to buy the Gizmat until you know what it does. As soon as I say "The Gizmat attaches to your gas tank and makes sure you get 100 miles to the gallon," you know what it does, and you can make a decision as to whether you want to buy it.

Now I'm going to confuse you a bit. Suppose you saw two Gizmats together. One was made by the Dooz company, and the other made by the Schmooze company, they both look the same, and they both say you'll get 100 miles a gallon. Now which one do you buy?

Impossible to know.

Unless! Unless one of them tells you more than the other about what the product will do for you (the buyer). "Never needs repair." "Never rusts." "Works to 40 below zero." "Saves money on gas." "Paint never chips," are all either **direct benefits** (you can see the benefits right away. For example: "Save money on gas" is a pretty clear, understandable benefit. It means you're not going to spend as much money on gas as you used to, which means you ultimately save money, which means you have more money to spend on other things. "Saving money on gas," therefore, is an excellent benefit.)...

...or they're **indirect benefits** (you *can't* see the benefits right away; they're a little hidden. For example, "Never needs repair" is a benefit to the buyer that's a little harder to grasp. Sure, you never need to repair the

Gizmat, but what are the actual benefits of that? Well, I can think of *lots* of them: for instance, there will never be a day that your car will be in the shop on account of the Gizmat; the Gizmat will be good for a lifetime; you'll be able to take it from one car to another; you can count on the quality; you'll have confidence in the company that made it, etc.)

If you look at both the direct and indirect benefits, they are the reasons why you might buy something. Remember, you didn't want to buy the Gizmat before you knew what it did for you, but then you were more inclined to buy it once you learned how it would benefit *you*.

Here's another example. This is my favorite one. Imagine you're old enough to have a couple of kids (8 and 10), and suppose you've been traveling for five hours and the kids are a little tired, but *very* hungry. You come over the brow of a hill and see a McDonalds and a Joe's Grill.

Where are you most likely to stop to eat?

I'll take a wild guess and say probably McDonalds. I ask all my workshop and class participants this same question, and they almost always say McDonalds.

Then I ask them why. You try it.

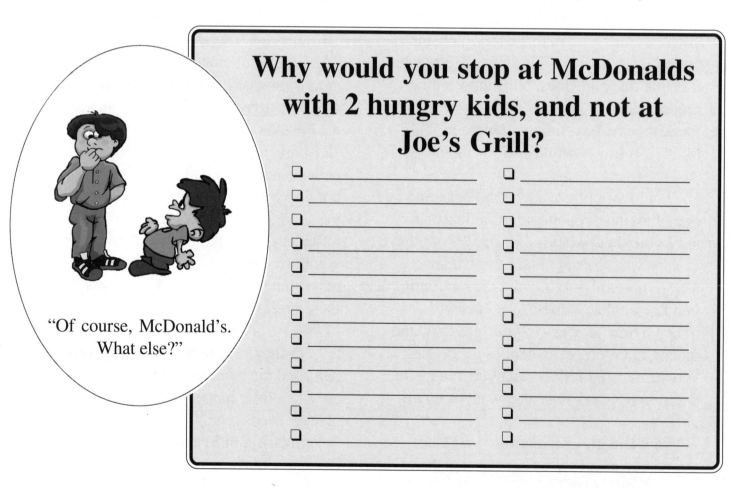

"Of course, McDonald's. What else?"

Why would you stop at McDonalds with 2 hungry kids, and not at Joe's Grill?

❑ ____________________ ❑ ____________________
❑ ____________________ ❑ ____________________
❑ ____________________ ❑ ____________________
❑ ____________________ ❑ ____________________
❑ ____________________ ❑ ____________________
❑ ____________________ ❑ ____________________
❑ ____________________ ❑ ____________________
❑ ____________________ ❑ ____________________
❑ ____________________ ❑ ____________________
❑ ____________________ ❑ ____________________
❑ ____________________ ❑ ____________________
❑ ____________________ ❑ ____________________

There's a good chance you wrote down many of the following reasons for stopping at McDonalds:

- The bathrooms are clean
- They have Happy Meals.
- They have toys.
- Their food is consistently good.
- You know what to expect.
- They're fast.
- They're inexpensive.
- They have a kids play area.
- There are a lot of other kids there, so you don't have to worry about making noise.
- It's easy to get back on the highway.
- They have a lot of choices for things to eat.
- They have good things to drink.
- There's no smoking.
- There's always a place to park.
- Your kids probably already know what they want.
- You know your kids won't complain.

Do you know that in all my public speaking engagements, no one has *ever* mentioned the actual food? No one has said "We stop at McDonalds because the burgers are out of this world." Or "the fries are to die for." Or "the McNuggets are unbelievably delicious."

Nope! All they care about is stopping at McDonalds for all the benefits that have nothing to do with the food itself. Isn't that amazing?

So what does McDonalds do in their advertising? They emphasize those benefits. They tie themselves in to everything Disney's doing (Doug was a big deal, and so was Toy Story), they emphasize happy meals for the kids, they talk about grilling the burgers, they have unbelievable discounts. At the end of '99, their marketing campaign is all about D&D, Discounting and Disney, and nothing about their food.

Is that amazing or what?

The reason I'm spending some time on this, is that if there's anything I'd wish you to remember when you get done with this book, it's the fact that people do *not* buy the actual product or service; they buy the benefits the product or service brings to them.

Think about the McDonalds example above.

Now the tricky part is to do this for your *own* product/service. Suppose you're running a school store. Or you're an attorney. Or you make a floor sweeping compound. Or you're a comedian. What you need to market are the benefits you'll bring your potential customers. All your letters, brochures, business cards, posters, flyers, contents of your web page, your answering machine message, your 8 second response when someone asks what you do -- essentially everything you use to tell other people what you do/offer -- has to emphasize these benefits.

It is *very* difficult to figure out these benefits, but it's well worth it. To make it a little easier, I've designed what I call my "**benefits wheels**." Take a look at them and see if you can figure them out.

The box in the center is where you note the product/service. Let's say it's one of those Ginsu knives that's advertised on late night TV.

I have shown only three wheels, but there could be many more. Follow the first arrow to the right wheel, and in the center write down one of the *features* of this knife. Let's say "Never needs sharpening." Now go out to the first, small ring near the center of the circle and try thinking of three benefits of this knife never needing sharpening.

Try (1) always stays sharp, (2) no special sharpening tools needed, (3) less likely to cut yourself, as it won't slip off the food.

Now go out to the next larger ring and try to think of at least two benefits for each of the three benefits above. I'll just take the "always stays sharp" benefit and ask myself "What're two benefits of the knife always staying sharp? (1) I'll never have to sharpen it again, (2) It will always cut right the first time.

Now go out to the third ring and try to think of at least two benefits for each of the two benefits above. I'll take the "I'll never have to sharpen it again" benefit and ask myself "What're two benefits of never having to sharpen that knife again? (1) I'll save time, (2) I'll never worry again. Here's a third one: I'll save money.

These benefits, the ones you list on this third ring, are the benefits that motivate people to make decisions to spend money. If you're accurate in thinking through and making out these benefits wheels, you will have discovered why people will buy your product/service. These benefits, the ones on the third ring, are the ones that you must use in your marketing efforts to sell whatever it is that you're selling.

try them out

Service/Product Benefits Wheels

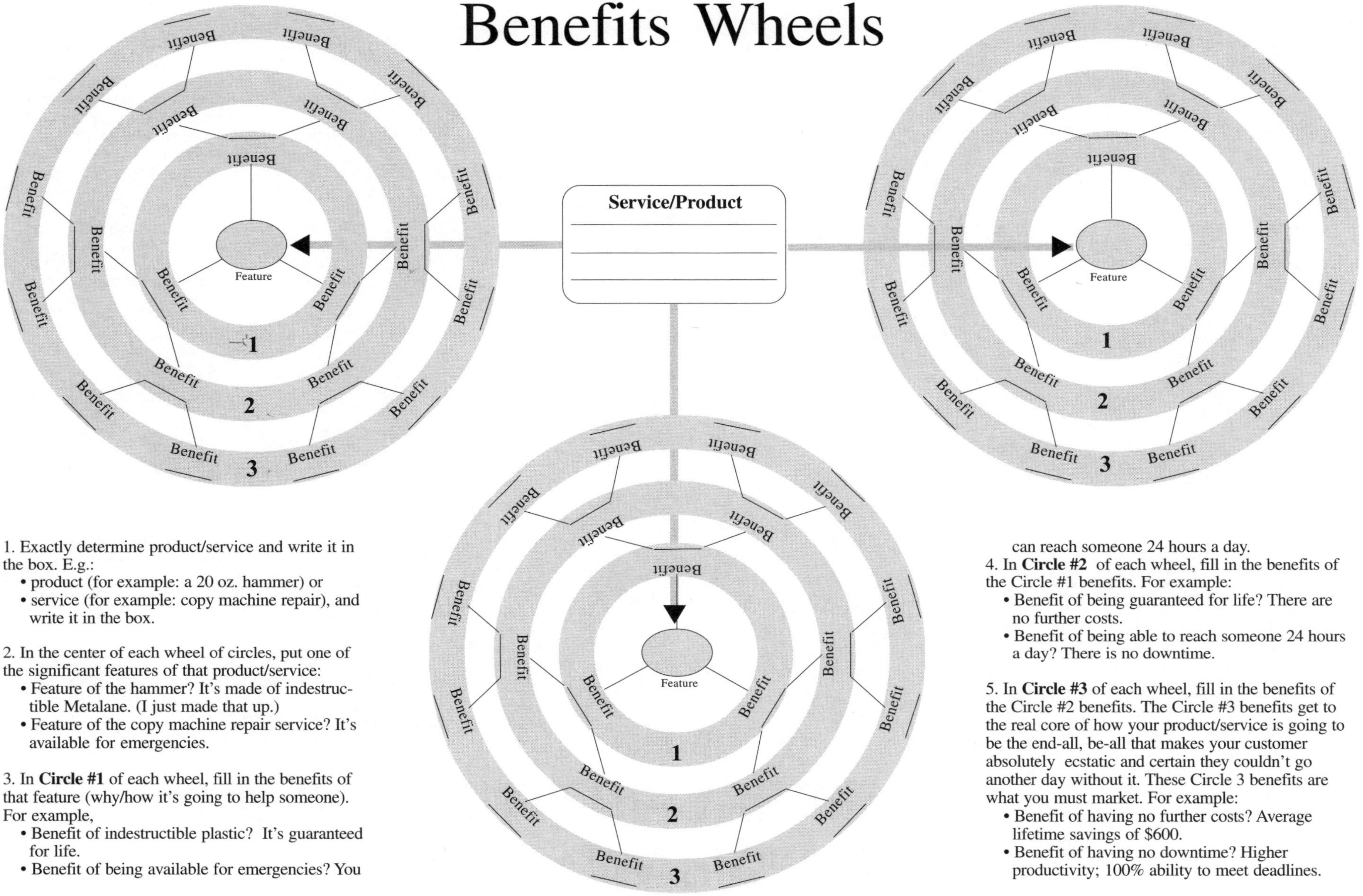

1. Exactly determine product/service and write it in the box. E.g.:
   - product (for example: a 20 oz. hammer) or
   - service (for example: copy machine repair), and write it in the box.

2. In the center of each wheel of circles, put one of the significant features of that product/service:
   - Feature of the hammer? It's made of indestructible Metalane. (I just made that up.)
   - Feature of the copy machine repair service? It's available for emergencies.

3. In **Circle #1** of each wheel, fill in the benefits of that feature (why/how it's going to help someone). For example,
   - Benefit of indestructible plastic? It's guaranteed for life.
   - Benefit of being available for emergencies? You can reach someone 24 hours a day.

4. In **Circle #2** of each wheel, fill in the benefits of the Circle #1 benefits. For example:
   - Benefit of being guaranteed for life? There are no further costs.
   - Benefit of being able to reach someone 24 hours a day? There is no downtime.

5. In **Circle #3** of each wheel, fill in the benefits of the Circle #2 benefits. The Circle #3 benefits get to the real core of how your product/service is going to be the end-all, be-all that makes your customer absolutely ecstatic and certain they couldn't go another day without it. These Circle 3 benefits are what you must market. For example:
   - Benefit of having no further costs? Average lifetime savings of $600.
   - Benefit of having no downtime? Higher productivity; 100% ability to meet deadlines.

Service/Product Benefits Wheels

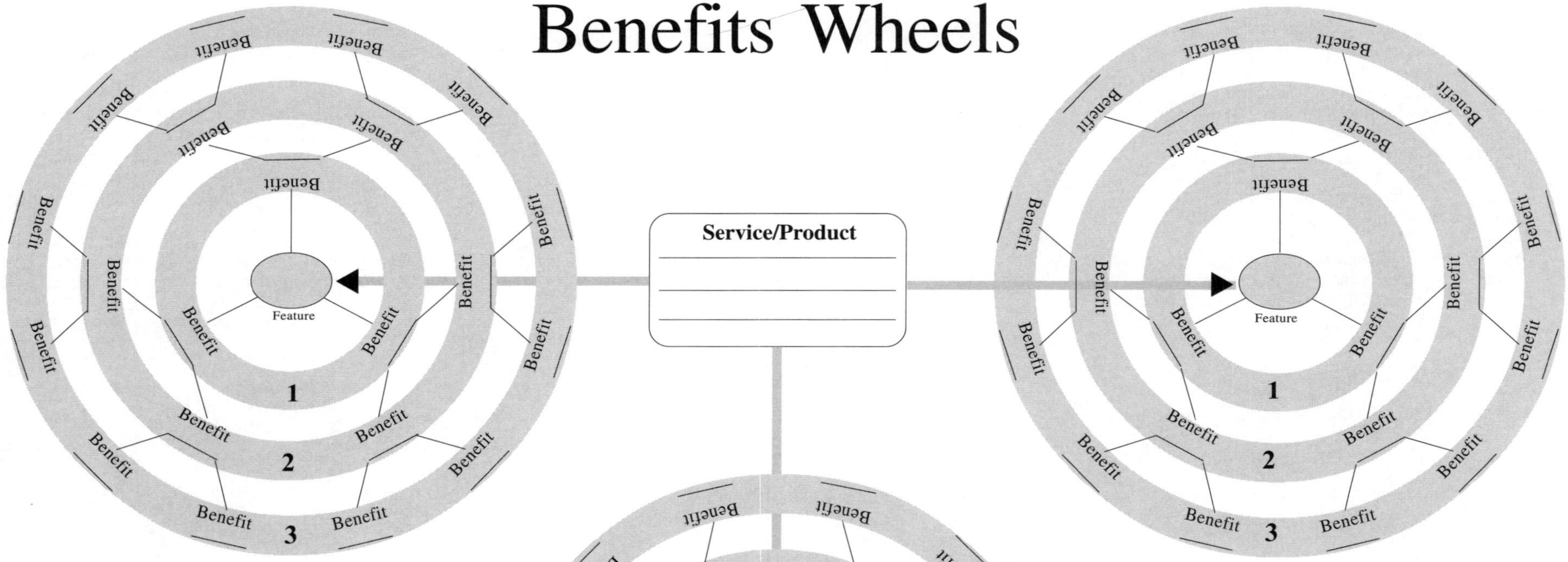

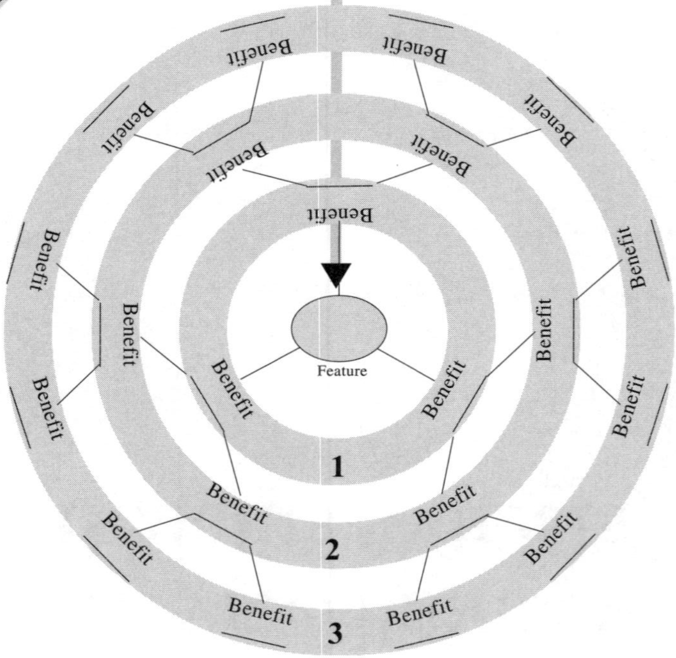

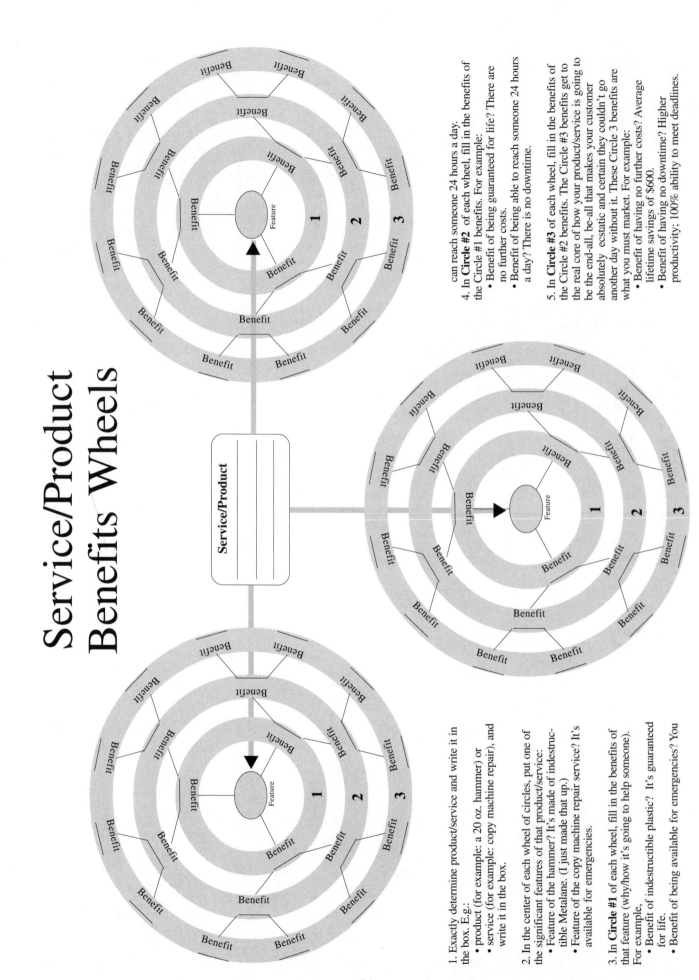

1. Exactly determine product/service and write it in the box. E.g.:
   - product (for example: a 20 oz. hammer) or
   - service (for example: copy machine repair), and write it in the box.

2. In the center of each wheel of circles, put one of the significant features of that product/service:
   - Feature of the hammer? It's made of indestructible Metalane. (I just made that up.)
   - Feature of the copy machine repair service? It's available for emergencies.

3. In **Circle #1** of each wheel, fill in the benefits of that feature (why/how it's going to help someone). For example,
   - Benefit of indestructible plastic? It's guaranteed for life.
   - Benefit of being available for emergencies? You can reach someone 24 hours a day.

4. In **Circle #2** of each wheel, fill in the benefits of the Circle #1 benefits. For example:
   - Benefit of being guaranteed for life? There are no further costs.
   - Benefit of being able to reach someone 24 hours a day? There is no downtime.

5. In **Circle #3** of each wheel, fill in the benefits of the Circle #2 benefits. The Circle #3 benefits get to the real core of how your product/service is going to be the end-all, be-all that makes your customer absolutely ecstatic and certain they couldn't go another day without it. These Circle 3 benefits are what you must market. For example:
   - Benefit of having no further costs? Average lifetime savings of $600.
   - Benefit of having no downtime? Higher productivity; 100% ability to meet deadlines.

What makes your *business* Unique?

Here are some individual characteristics that might make your ***business*** stand out from the crowd. You should

- Add to this list,
- Then figure out how you can market those qualities.

❑ I save you money	❑ ____________	❑ ____________
❑ I make you happier	❑ ____________	❑ ____________
❑ I make your business run smoother	❑ ____________	❑ ____________
❑ I'm available 24 hours a say	❑ ____________	❑ ____________
❑ I use the latest technology	❑ ____________	❑ ____________
❑ I'm current with the cutting edge	❑ ____________	❑ ____________
❑ My image is impeccable	❑ ____________	❑ ____________
❑ No one beats my response time	❑ ____________	❑ ____________
❑ I have an active URL	❑ ____________	❑ ____________
❑ I credit you for referrals	❑ ____________	❑ ____________
❑ A person answers my phone	❑ ____________	❑ ____________
❑ I'm exceptionally honest.	❑ ____________	❑ ____________
❑ ____________	❑ ____________	❑ ____________
❑ ____________	❑ ____________	❑ ____________

"I have the premier, foremost, best, leading, superb business in the region for (less than 25 words):

____

____

____
"

____

Now you're in a position to tell us exactly what you'll be marketing and exactly to whom!

The 8 Second Rule

The clearer you are about what you do, how you do it, and how your customer will benefit, the easier it is

- to be excited about it,
- to find the right people to tell it to, and
- to find the best *ways* to tell it.

Therefore, you need to find a way to explain what you do in enough detail so the layperson understands exactly the nature of your service/product, why it's different from every one else's, and how it could provide a benefit or help them solve a problem. Your verbal explanation should take no more than 8 -15 seconds (30 words; 2 sentences), the amount of time you have someone's attention after they say:

"So, what do *you* do for work?"

(combine everything from the previous pages, but make it even more succinct)

Exercise

PS: I know one person who spent months on this! So don't despair, and don't be afraid to change it after you try it out a few times!

Congratulations!

You have completed what marketing students call "positioning," which is essentially creating a niche no one else has.

You'll know for sure whether you've created this niche when your prospective customer ("the end user") *becomes* your customer. As a preliminary test, you can always ask a prospective customer or a group of prospective customers (a "focus group") what their reaction might be.

"I provide/sell ______ (Show them pictures, models, outcomes, if possible). If I offered you this service/product, would you buy it?

"Would you be willing to explain your reaction?"

Relationship Marketing

This next set of exercises go the next step. If you've done a good (Sorry. Not good. *Great*!) job defining your customer, your uniqueness, and the uniqueness of your product/service, the next step is to actually make the sale.

I'm not going to discuss sales techniques. Hundreds of books have been written on the art of selling and "closing the deal," but I *am* going to address something even more important: the relationship you establish with your potential customer prior to the sale.

"All your marketing needs to be focused on creating and maintaining relationships with customers."

Unless you're desperate, or unless you just don't care, you (I mean *you* and not someone else) only buy a product/service from someone you like, trust, feel good about, feel comfortable with, like the looks of, or have confidence in. Your customer is looking for that same relationship with you, so all your marketing needs to be focused on creating and maintaining that relationship.

The relationship, therefore, is key. The next few pages are designed to get you to think about that relationship so you can manage it to your benefit and to the benefit of your business.

The importance of
a positive relationship in the contracting process

"The more friendly and caring the interaction, the more satisfying the transaction."

Keep in mind that the buy-sell transaction must be a win-win situation. Your customer must walk away from the purchase with a "want" satisfied, and you need to walk away feeling good about what you offered and what you're being compensated.

So -- figuring out exactly what makes the "vendor-customer" relationship work -- in the beginning and over the long term -- will give you the edge you need to grow.

Exercise:

	What makes you feel "nicely treated" in a buy-sell relationship?	Why is it important in your marketing process?	Can you adopt it in your way of doing business?
1			
2			
3			
4			
5			
6			
7			
8			
9			
10			

We "trust" a vendor to sell us a good product or service, to be there if we have a problem later, to give the same level of service next time we come, and to give our friends the same good service.

Defining the trust factor

	What characteristics make someone trustworthy?	Which of these do you have for certain?	Are you making people aware of this characteristic?	How can you improve it to make a better impression of being "trustworthy?"
1				
2				
3				
4				
5				
6				
7				
8				
9				
10				

If you decide to work on making a better impression, you are implementing a part of your marketing plan

Do you trust this person to give you a *great* haircut?

PS: I know a therapist who realized she was getting large numbers of referrals from her hairdresser, so now one of her primary marketing strategies is taking her hairdresser to lunch frequently.

Let's take another look at your definition of marketing. With it in mind, and having just made your list of factors affecting the way in which you "treat" (deal with) your potential customers, and the factors that help them "trust" you as a potential providor of a product or service to them, try making a list of those things you are currently doing (or just now realized you were doing) to market your business.

See chart on next page →

What are you currently doing
to market your business?

	Using your definition, list here the things you are now doing that could be considered "marketing" (regardless of whether you think them good or bad).	Do you think they're working?	Why? or why not	Should you keep doing them?

This list should become part of your new marketing plan

What Do People Buy?

"They buy promises you make. So make them with care. * They buy the promises they want personally fulfilled. * They buy your credibility or don't buy if you lack it. * They buy solutions to their problems. * They buy you, your employees, your service department. * They buy wealth, safety, success, security, love and acceptance. * They buy your guarantee, reputation and good name. * They buy other people's opinions of your business. * They buy expectations based upon your marketing. * They buy believable claims, not simply honest claims. * They buy hope for their own and their company's future. * They buy brand names over strange names. * They buy the consistency they've seen you exhibit. * They buy the stature of the media in which you market. * They buy the professionalism of your marketing materials. * They buy value, which is not the same as price. * They buy selection and often the best of your selection. * They buy freedom from risk, granted by your warranty. * They buy acceptance by others of your goods or services. * They buy certainty. * They buy convenience in buying, paying and lots more. * They buy respect for their own ideas and personality. * They buy your identity as conveyed by your marketing. * They buy style -- just the kind that fits their own style. * They buy neatness and assume that's how you do business. * They buy easy access to information about you, offered by your website. * They buy honesty for one dishonest word means no sale. * They buy comfort, offerings that fit their comfort zone. * They buy success; your success can fit with theirs. * They buy good taste and know it from bad taste. * They buy instant gratification and don't love to wait. * They buy the confidence you display in your own business. It's also important to know what customers do not buy: fancy adjectives, exaggerated claims, clever headlines, special effects, marketing that screams, marketing that even hints at amateurishness, the lowest price anything (though 14 percent do), unproven items, or gorgeous graphics that get in the way of the message." from http://www.gmarketing.com

"People don't buy things, like products and services. They buy results like happiness, making and saving money, saving time, popularity, wisdom, comfort, recognition, attractiveness, safety, security, and easier ways to do things." Dan McComas

Finding Customers

You are currently doing some things to "market" your business, and clearly those activities are directed at someone.

Remember we said that one definition of marketing was "anything you do that lets someone else know what you do."

You could, of course, let people know who wouldn't be of any help to you.

For instance, you could be marketing to someone you hope will refer a lot of people to you. Turns out that person has an allegiance to one of your strongest competitors, so you've wasted a lot of time.

Or you decided to spend lots of dollars advertising in the yellow pages because you were convinced that young, upscale adults look there for ideas about buying the kind of product/service you offer. Turns out, young adults rely more on the advice of their friends working out at the "Y" than they do the Yellow Pages, so you've obviously wasted your money.

Clearly, you would like to focus your attention and limited resources only on those areas and individuals meeting your criteria for potential customers.

How would you do that?

Who are your customers?

"Where will my new customers come from?"

"And who are they?"

Numerous marketing studies over the past decade show that the best source of new business is **existing customers**. Second best is **referrals** (a function of networking).

It's the same story, whether trying to determine what new products or services to offer, or trying to increase the size of your business. Your existing customers and referral sources are your best bet, hands down. Hands down!

Complete the chart below to find out the sources of your referrals (where your customers came from, how they found out about you, where they heard about you).

Customer		A colleague	Another customer	Friend	Trade show	Advertising	Cold call	Returning customer	"Leads" group	walk-in (or "out-of-the-blue")	Attorneys	You generated the lead	From Being on a Committee	"Rubber chicken" circuit	Seminar/workshop	Part of a trade group	Tradeshow	Mailing	Website	Email contact	Other ______
1																					
2																					
3																					
4																					
5																					
6																					
7																					
8																					
9																					
10																					
Compile totals here. Develop better relationships with referral sources with the highest totals!																					

Be Nice to Your Sources

Based on the previous chart, list each of your sources here, and figure out how you might get more business from them -- in a way that's comfortable for you!

Have you thanked people? Can you schedule meetings with them to talk about other ways you can help them? Can you mention them in your newsletter? Send referrals their way? Can you give away something meaningful at the next trade show that reminds prospective customers about something of yours that's special? Should you increase the size of your ad? Join another leads group? Volunteer more time to highly visible community groups? (See "Referrals" later in the workbook.)

The source	What did you do to get the work/order?	What can you do to get more from this source?
Referrals		
1		
2		
3		
Advertising (where?)		
1		
2		
3		
Leads group		
1		
2		
3		
Volunteer		
1		
2		
3		
Other person/thing		
1		
2		
3		
4		
5		
6		
7		
8		
9		

Here's an interesting note .... about why it's important to be nice to your referral sources (who are essentially advocates for your business).

"The way (referral sources)
judge a service
may depend as much or even more
*on the service **process***
*than on the service **outcome**!"*

Texas A&M Professor Len Berry

The following relates to a doctor-patient relationship, but the message can apply to the relationships you have with your referral sources, as well.

An experiment was conducted by Australian physician M.H.N. Tattersall on the effect of office procedures on patients. 48 were randomly broken into 2 groups, Half got follow-up letters, half didn't. While **13** of the ones who got the letters were "completely satisfied," only **4** of the other group had the same response -- **a difference of almost 40%!**

What made that difference? The letter changed the perception of the visit. With the letter, the doctor showed additional interest and made the clients feel like their doctor was attempting to strike up a closer, caring relationship with them.

The doctor had practiced the beginnings of "relationship marketing." There's a good chance the group who got the letters will tell more people how caring their doctor is, which is obviously great for the growth of Tattersall's business.

Marketing Strategies Used by Consultants

	(7,005 consultants surveyed) Strategy	How many consultants used this?	How many of these had incomes less than $409K?	How many of these had incomes greater than $75K?	Strategy ranking
1	Promotion to similar clients on basis of referrals or names obtained from other customers.	42.1%	25.6%	57.4%	6
2	Lectures to civic, trade, and professional audiences	18.8	6.2	37.8	5
3	Writing articles, books, newsletters for trade, professional, and civic audiences	16.3	8.8	28.1	4
4	Providing free assessment services to pre-qualified leads	45.2	66.6	23.7	3
5	Direct mailing of brochures/ marketing letters to cold lists	58.9	68.3	17.9	2
6	Cold personal calls	54.4	75.3	15.8	1

source unknown

Note that 57% of consultants with the highest incomes relied on marketing programs involving referrals and their sources!

Another Survey of Strategies

Marketing methods used by consultants	Average effectiveness	Percent using this method	Percent planning to use this method next year
Getting repeat business	**8**	93.2	90.9
Getting referrals	**7**	**79.5**	**84.1**
Networking	**6**	79.5	77.3
Giving free consultations	**5**	**43.2**	**50.0**
Writing artilces	**5**	**36.6**	**52.3**
Giving seminars	4	29.5	27.3
Advertising	4	29.5	27.3
Making cold calls	3	**27.3**	**34.1**
Responding to gov. RFPs	4	22.7	18.2
Sending direct mail	4	**20.4**	**31.8**
Sending press releases	5	**18.2**	**43.2**
Sending newsletters	5	**15.9**	**22.7**
Exhibiting at trade shows	4	**11.4**	**20.4**
Using an 800 number	5	unk	unk

source unknown

Note that 93% of consultants relied on getting business from existing clients, and that marketing to them had the highest effectiveness rating (8). Marketing programs designed around "getting referrals" and used by 84% of all consultants had the second highest effectiveness rating (7)!

Two steps for Increasing

Sales to Existing Customers

1. Recognize and Pay Attention to *them*

- Send *handwritten* thank you notes.
- Give them a gift certificate, flower for their office, or other small present.
- Send them referrals.
- Send birthday/holiday cards to them or members of their families, or copy of an article you know they'll enjoy.
- If they're nearby, visit them. Some reasons to visit?
  - You want to find out more about *their* business so you can provide them with more applicable services.
  - You developed a new handout about a new product/service that might help *them*, and you would love to have their input before printing it.
  - You want to replenish the handouts in their office, or give them your new business card.
  - You want to personally thank them for trusting you enough to send referrals your way.
  - You want to introduce your new personal assistant, or new colleague or associate.
  - You changed offices and want to hand deliver an invitation to your open house.
  - You want to demonstrate your new service/product.
  - ____________________
  - ____________________
  - ____________________
  - ____________________
  - ____________________
  - ____________________
  - ____________________
  - ____________________
  - ____________________
  - ____________________
  - ____________________
  - ____________________

A Customer Appreciation Program

What can I say? You need to take care of your existing customers. For lots of reasons. First, it takes a long time and costs a lot of money to get them in the first place. Second, at least 70% of your business will come from existing customers, so these people represent your future cash flow. If you know these two things, then why *wouldn't* you figure out some way to thank customers and keep them coming back once you have them? If you take good care of them, they'll be back time and time again, and look *forward* to it!

Developing a powerful customer appreciation program doesn't take a lot of skill or money, but it *does* take careful thought about what kind of time and money you *can* afford.

Don't compare what you can do to what huge companies do. Customers really don't care how much money you spend on them. You *can*, though, do something the big guys can't. You can tailor your program. You can make each customer feel as though they're getting special treatment. Examples? Partner with another business to bring your customers something they wouldn't think about doing for themselves, like asking your computer store friend to give your customers a live demonstration in your office of new software which could help them. Or around holidays, send them cards and a special greeting, or a dozen donuts for their office, or have pizza delivered, or a plant for their spring garden.

If you can tie the theme in with your own products/services, even better. That is, rather than purchase promotional items from some company, figure out what you can produce/offer that reflects your own products/services. If you're a marketing consultant, for instance, you could send them calendars you put together at Kinkos on which you put periodic marketing tips.

Just be creative, frequent, and consistent. And then keep track of what made the best impression so you can do it again.

2. Get More Business From Them

- Bend over backwards to add value to your services so your clients will report good things back to the person who referred them.
- Make absolutely sure you're on time for appointments.
- If they ask, refer customers to other helpful professionals.
- Make a point to know about a customer's interests; send relevant articles or notes.
- Offer to collaborate.
- If you constantly analyze *their* business, and you discover you could provide a service that would make *their* clients' lives easier, develop the service and offer it to them.
- Give them a reason to tell someone (a potential customer or another referral source) about your business.
- Do *whatever* is necessary to encourage word of mouth. Think what you can do that will be so amazing, so nice, so wonderful, so thoughtful, so memorable, that they'll tell a friend or someone else who could send you referrals.
- Develop materials or a system that would make it easy for a referral source to convey information to *their* customers about *your* business (brochures, leaflets, posters...).
- Ask them for more referrals! Asking for business always generates more business, but the question is rarely asked.
- ____
- ____
- ____
- ____
- ____
- ____
- ____
- ____

Part
2

The Marketing Plan

Your Marketing Plan

Excuse the schmaltz, please, but you *are* at the point of putting together a marketing plan for your business.

It's really easy, and by now you've probably already done it, but just in case you haven't had the courage, let's try putting one together now.

The development of your product/service is entirely based on what your potential customers told you they want/need. If you've done your research properly, you may already have a good idea of your potential customer's profile.

Because a marketing plan must accurately reflect that profile, use the following exercise to help make sure you're targeting the right people.

Your Step by Step Marketing Plan

A marketing plan is part of the process of developing a Business Plan, so if you've done your homework for the business plan, many of the decisions about your marketing plan have already been made.

The step-by-step for developing a marketing plan is pretty simple:

1. Identify potential customers

____

____

____

____

____

____

____

____

1. Identify a potential customer.

Because of the nature of your product/ service, you may, in fact, have several different kinds of customers. For instance, if you're selling a pet sitting service, your customers may be traveling families, invalids, and kennels that overflow. If you're selling legal workshops, your customers may be law firms, individual practitioners, legal training providers, and other workshop leaders.

You should obviously make this list of potential customers and rank them in some order of importance, but then it's a good idea to develop a separate marketing plan for each. They don't need to be long; just one page will do. But each deserves a special look to see whether they should be catered to a little differently from the others.

1a. Pick One to target!

____

2. Contact the potential customer.

Buying something always involves a *process*. People just don't leap out of bed one morning and announce that they're going to buy a new pair of sneakers or a new car. That *rarely* happens. Think back to the last time you bought a pair of sneakers. Obviously it'll be a little different for everyone, but your process probably went something like this:

You've had your sneakers for 8 months, you wear them every day, and they're starting to look a little worn. It used to be they were so new, and looked so good, that you just put them on without thinking. Now you start noticing how worn they are. One day, you have to get dressed up a *little* more than usual, and when you put on your sneakers, you notice how worn they really are. "I should probably get a new pair of sneakers one of these days," you say to yourself, and then you start noticing other people's new sneaks. Or you start paying attention to the sales ads in the paper. Or you overhear someone saying they just bought a pair at Footlocker. You begin wondering whether you can afford them now, anyway. Then you "find" a little extra money.

Then -- well, a number of other things or thoughts may happen, but eventually, you end up buying some new sneakers.

Look at the process you went through! If you're buying a car or a house, the process is even more involved.

The point is, when someone is thinking about buying your product/service, they are going to go through a process. If they're buying a can of soda from your store, the process is pretty simple and probably has more to do with habit than anything else, but they still go through a process.

Once you put on your marketing cap, you need to think about the process your potential customers are going to go through before they buy what you're selling, and then you need to affect that process. You need to feed into it in some fashion. You need to put something in the way so your customers will essentially stumble over it on their way to buying. You need to become part of their process.

So -- back to **#2 Contact the potential customer.** Once you think through their buying process, what's the best way to influence it? Don't forget that you want to emphasize the benefits. It might go something like this:

"Just as I know they're running out of a competitor's product, I will contact potential customer X by sending them a letter and a brochure about my product's benefits."

How will you contact the customer you identified in **1a**?

I will contact **Customer 1a** in the following manner:

3. Figure out the strategy for making the sale.

- A week later, I will follow up with a phone call with the idea of making an appointment to show them how my product will benefit them enormously
- I'll bring them a sample.
- I'll ask for the sale.
- I'll put them on my database and send them periodic announcements about sales, or about product changes.
- Every time they buy my product, I'll acknowledge them in some way.
- I'll encourage them to refer me to other, similar customers, and if they do, I'll thank them by giving them a discount on their next purchase.

What's your Strategy?

Worksheet for Potential Customers

Use one per potential customer

Who is the potential customer? Name of individual or group	
How many potential customers are there in the targeted group? Does this number make it worth your while?	
What need(s) of theirs can you meet with the benefits of your product/service?	
Given your competition, what chance is there that the potential customer will buy what you're offering?	
Profile (list the characteristics) of your idea potential customer. What would you prefer they have? Examples **gender** **age** **income** **education** **type of business** **Position** **be an existing customer** **location** **credit rating** **technologically proficient** **gross sales** **ISO qualified** **team-based organization**	
Does the potential customer in #1 match this profile?	
If you targeted a group (individuals or companies), how many customers can you get from this group (market share)?	
What's the best way to find this potential customer? **referral? (from whom?)** **mailing** **trade show** **visit** **fax offer** **email contact** **website** **letter writing/material sending strategy** **other** **other**	
Exactly what will your strategy be to get this customer? (list the steps)	
Do you need to develop materials? What?	
How much time do you need to commit?	
How much money will it take? Will you commit it?	
What's your deadline?	

Here's a really Simple Marketing Plan

Remember I said that a Marketing Plan is a formally prepared document that identifies potential customers, determines the best way to reach them (the strategies), and details exactly what you're going to do to make the strategies work.

To give you an idea of the level of detail, here's an example for an in-home pet sitting service:

1 Identify a potential customer. I have identified pet owners with household incomes of more than $75,000 as one group of potential customers.

2 Determine the best way to reach them. I will reach them through their veterinarians.

3 Exactly what am I going to do to make this strategy work?

1. I will find out which veterinarians see this group of people.
2. Then I'll develop two sets of materials I can leave at the Vets' offices after I meet with them.
   a. One will be designed to give them information that helps them feel comfortable with my services and OK about referring me.
   b. The other will be an educational piece that can be left in their waiting room that is eye-appealing and designed to attract the interest of people going on trips.
3. Then I'll make an appointment with the 3 veterinarians I feel most comfortable visiting, meet with them, and review the benefits of my services with them.
4. After the meeting, I'll send a note thanking them for their time and responding to any questions they may have raised during our meeting.
5. Then I'll make a note on my calendar to occasionally replenish their offices with the handouts and business cards, and to either say "hi" if they're available, or leave a note on *my* note paper (it has my logo and paw prints all over it) telling them I was there.
6. Then I'll make sure to send them thank you notes when they send me referrals.
8. I'll set up a way to track the success of this strategy so I know whether to keep it for next year.

What's *Your*

Simple Marketing Plan

look like?

Try filling this out for your business. Use the previous plans to help guide your filling in the blanks.

1 Identify a potential customer.
I have identified __________ with ______________________ as one group of potential customers.

2 Determine the best way to reach them.
I will reach them through ______________________.

3 Exactly what am I going to do to make this strategy work?

1. I will find out which ______________ see this group of people.
2. Then I'll develop _______ sets of materials I can leave at their office after I meet with them.
   a. One will be designed to give them information that helps them feel comfortable with my services/products and OK about referring me.
   b. The other will be an educational piece that can be left in their waiting room that is eye-appealing and designed to attract the interest of people ____________.
3. Then I'll make an appointment with _________________ I feel most comfortable visiting, meet with them, and review my services/products with them.
4. After the meeting, I'll send a note thanking them for their time and responding to any questions they may have raised during our meeting.
5. Then I'll make a note on my calendar to occasionally replenish their offices with the handouts and business cards, and to either say "hi" if they're available, or leave a note on *my* note paper telling them I was there.
6. Then I'll make sure to send them thank you notes when they send me referrals.
7. Then I'll ________________________
____
____
____
____
8. Then I'll ________________________
____
____
____
____
9. I'll set up a way to track the success of this strategy so I know whether to keep it for next year.

On the following page, entrepreneurs/students can develop a marketing plan for a business they have in mind.

Here's another variation! Feel free to fill this one in. There's another copy on the next page.

Marketing Plan for

____

1 Which customer (existing or potential) would you like to go after? (See your Worksheet)

What exactly will you be marketing to this customer ? (See your previous exercise)

2 What do you want to tell this customer about your product or service? (See "What makes you unique?" exercise, and add concrete info about your service/product).

3 What's the best **format(s)** for presenting your information (verbal, letter, brochure, flyer, combination)?

4 Do you have it available already, or do you have to compose it, print it?

5 Once you've decided the format(s), detail the exact strategy you'll use to get the information in the customer's hand/head. (See the previous "What's a Simple Marketing Plan look like?")

6 The Costs. Depending on what your plan and strategy look like, there may or may not be costs that need to be identified. If there are, list them and make sure you can afford them.

7 Calculate how much time you think needs to be allocated for:
- getting your information ready?
- carrying out all the parts of your strategy?

8 Do you have the time? If so, put on your calendar the deadline dates for every piece of your plan and strategy.

9 The last thing? Put a start date here:

(Feel free to copy this form for your personal use.)

Marketing Plan for

____

1 Which customer (existing or potential) would you like to go after? (See your Worksheet)

What exactly will you be marketing to this customer ? (See your previous exercise)

2 What do you want to tell this customer about your product or service? (See "What makes you unique?" exercise, and add concrete info about your service/product).

3 What's the best **format(s)** for presenting your information (verbal, letter, brochure, flyer, combination)?

4 Do you have it available already, or do you have to compose it, print it?

5 Once you've decided the format(s), detail the exact strategy you'll use to get the information in the customer's hand/head. (See the previous "What's a Simple Marketing Plan look like?")

6 The Costs. Depending on what your plan and strategy look like, there may or may not be costs that need to be identified. If there are, list them and make sure you can afford them.

7 Calculate how much time you think needs to be allocated for:

- getting your information ready?
- carrying out all the parts of your strategy?

8 Do you have the time? If so, put on your calendar the deadline dates for every piece of your plan and strategy.

9 The last thing? Put a start date here: ____________________

Part 3

Mini-Marketing Plans

The Concept of Guerilla Marketing

"The need for guerrilla marketing can be seen in the light of three facts: Because of big business downsizing, decentralization, relaxation of government regulations, affordable technology, and a revolution in consciousness, people around the world are gravitating to small business in record numbers.

"Small business failures are also establishing record numbers and one of the main reasons for the failures is a failure to understand marketing.

"Guerrilla marketing has been proven in action to work for small businesses around the world. It works because it's simple to understand, easy to implement and outrageously inexpensive. Guerrilla marketing is needed because it gives small businesses a delightfully unfair advantage: certainty in an uncertain world, economy in a high-priced world, simplicity in a complicated world, marketing awareness in a clueless world."

From the Guerilla Marketing website: http:www.gmarketing.com

Mini Marketing Plans for

- Attitude
- Marketing Plan Strategies
- Image
- Customer Service
- Referrals
- Keeping in Touch
- PR/Advertising
- Office Procedures
- Electronic Communication
- Technology
- The Business
- Staying Current

Small but ***very*** effective...

"Your business has many components, each of which needs to be marketed."

This part of the book is neat because it gives you an easy way to start your marketing process.

Every business is comprised of several components, each of which needs to be marketed at one level or another. It's important to recognize the distinction between the marketing of these components, and the marketing of your actual product or service. For instance, the kind of customer service you provide has *nothing* to do with your product, nor does the way your phone is answered. Glance through the next several pages just to get a sense of what I'm talking about, then come back here.

Once you identify these numerous components, it's easy to develop Mini Marketing Plans for each of them, and to then implement those mini plans at your own pace and within your own stylistic abilities.

There are twelve (12) business components in the following pages, and within each are numerous small, but effective Mini Marketing Plans. What's nice about this approach is that you can implement the mini plans yourself (no doubt you'll have several going at once like I do). And because they can be broken out separately, you might be able to find other people to help you out, as well.

I can't repeat often enough that marketing is merely doing *something* that lets others know what you do. Only after you start will you have a sense of priorities, and they won't be the same for everyone. Depending on your daily mood, energy level, cash flow, and time, they may not be the same for you, either.

I always have several of these mini plans on my desk/calendar at any one time, because I know my interests change from day to day (well, actually from minute to minute). At the beginning of each week, I look through all my appointments and obligations, try to get a handle on what kind of marketing I feel like doing, then choose the mini plans that fit in. Some of them I'll repeat frequently; others I may never get to, but I rest assured knowing I'm doing *something* every week that helps my business grow.

Small but ***very*** effective...(continued)

If I have a major project (like marketing this book, or putting together a workshop, or designing a new flyer for my services), it may be my only marketing activity for weeks on end. If I've made a heavy financial commitment to one of the Mini Marketing Plans (a new brochure, for instance), I may lay low for a while and just do some follow-up work, or plan my next strategy.

Because these next sections will help you "tie it all together," let me take a moment to tell you the thinking that's behind them.

As I've said in other places in the book, there are really two parts to your marketing activities that need to be managed: the business part (number 1) and the service/product part (number 2). They go hand-in-hand; one can't survive without the other, but I've separated them this way because you need to understand that there's a whole other level of activities that will make or break your business besides whether your service or product is any good.

To give you an example. Suppose your product was the world's best. A prospective customer hears about it, calls your 800 number, it rings 15 times, no one answers. They're frustrated, but they try again later. The phone rings 12 times this time before Jane picks up the phone:

"PorterLockwoodBestProductontheMarketHelpYa?" she asks, bored.

"I just heard about your great product and would like some information," says the potential customer.

"Address?"

"127 Lockober Drive"

"Whaaat?" (annoyed) "Lockover?"

Whew. Lost me. I'm hanging up, already. I don't need that kind of abuse from anybody, much less the person answering the phone who's supposed to be representing the company and presenting a friendly, relationship-building image so I end up liking the image and buying the product.

The way that phone was answered had nothing to do with the product. Nor would the letterhead, the sign out front, the thank-you notes, the business card, the billing procedures, the way in which orders are fulfilled, or all those other things that support the way in which the product/service -- or its image -- is managed on behalf of the customer.

But these are all parts of the business that need to be marketed,

Small but ***very*** effective...(continued)

and marketed well, with a plan, a strategy, a budget, and a commitment.

These marketing activities are generic to any business.

Then there's the product/service that needs to be marketed. Researching the market for the actual product, determining the target market size, learning about market share, assessing the competition, identifying methods for reaching and then communicating with the target market, testing the market, and assessing the abilities and resources needed to conduct, maintain, and grow the business, are all factors that need to be addressed in some way. Part 2 is the section where we do this.

Some time ago I said that marketing is really an intentional process. This is the part I was talking about. But before you get all bogged down, throw your hands up, and say "See? I *knew* there was something about marketing I really hated! I can't *believe* he tells me *now*!!"

If you already have a business that's working, or you already have a product/service that's selling, don't panic! Part 3 is sort of for you, but only if you want to confirm some stuff and maybe get more serious about some things. I explain how each section of the outline affects both the research and process of marketing, so there's a good chance you'll learn new information that will help you refine ideas you now have about marketing your business.

Part 4, the "Marketing Your Service or Product" part, is primarily for those people who have an idea for a product/service, haven't thought it through yet, and need a reality check about what they're getting in to.

Whether you've been in business a while or are new to the whole idea, you should familiarize yourself with Part 4 and use it to the extent you need it.

And Part 5, "What to do next," is a quick overview that gives you a starting point and some order to your activities.

But now, let's get started with Part 3!

MiniPlans for the Attitude Component of Your Business

Your attitude about yourself and your business is probably the single-most important factor that will contribute to your success or failure. Here are some little mini-plans that will eventually pay off big time:

- ❑ Business is up and down, so if you're not prepared to ride the waves, you're out of luck. But if you're in, make sure you're IN!

- ❑ Keeping a **positive attitude** through thick and thin is more difficult as an entrepreneur, because typically you have no one off of whom you can bounce ideas (concerns, misgivings, horror stories). This is why coaches, mentors, and advisory groups have begun to sprout. They act as silent partners but have no financial interests in your company. Many of my clients use me as an "executive coach," "management counselor," or "marketing mentor," to talk about marketing or business, just so they don't feel so alone. We set up weekly appointments and then conduct conferences by phone. They last an hour to an hour and a half, and can take place any time of the day or night.

- ❑ **Success avoidance**: Being successful means having to make trade-offs, many of which you may not be willing to make. As an example, if you knew that by doing X you would be guaranteed to make a million dollars, would you do it?

  "Well, it depends on what X is," you say. For instance, if X meant you had to move to a new country, away your immediate family, you might say "No." Or if X meant you had to work 100 hours a week for the next 8 years, you might say "No way!" Or if X meant that, starting tomorrow, you'd have the entire burden of running a corporation with 4,000 employees, you might say "I don't think so.

Your Attitude (continued)

I'm not ready for that yet." Or, well, you know what I mean.

Another, more subtle example: if you own a small business, and you just figured out that the only way for you to be successful is to do things you think are unethical, there's a good chance you won't do them.

Here are some other things success may lead to, and you may consciously (or subconsciously) want to avoid many of them: an expectation that it continue, less freedom to make mistakes, supervisory responsibilities, job loyalty, upward mobility, pressure to conform, increased competition, a "career" vs. a "job," more money and/or higher status, increased travel, power or perceived power, increased stress, becoming more visible, being viewed as better than average, the envy of others, more of a focus on work, less time for other things, change in image, the unknown.

How do you deal with all this? Just remember that part of the success-avoidance phenomenon says that with every gain (in this case, the prospect of success) there are losses. Just knowing this may be enough to help you lighten up on yourself while you (and your staff, if you have one) make time for recognizing and understanding these losses before you go forward.

Your Attitude (continued)

- ❑ **Impostor Syndrome**: If people begin lauding you with all kinds of praise, and they begin having expectations of you, asking you to join boards, seeking your advice about all kinds of things, you might have a flash like "Do they really want *my* opinion? I think someone else could answer that question better than I can. They think I know more than I do. I hope no one finds out that I haven't been doing this for very long, because I don't really know what I'm doing. Look at that! They just paid me a thousand bucks! *Anybody* could have done *that*!"

  All part of the same syndrome, and it keeps you from taking credit when it's due, or from having a confident image and attitude.

  Now that you know about the impostor syndrome, whenever you begin saying these things to yourself ("I think they're pointing to the guy behind me"), you can smile, take credit silently or out loud, and move on.

- ❑ Speaking about attitude: Some years ago, a shoe company sent two salesmen to Africa to develop the market. After the first day of work, the first salesman wired home, "I'm coming home, no one here wears shoes". The second salesman wired home, "Send more salesmen, no one here wears shoes."

MiniPlans for the Marketing Plan Component of Your Business

- ❑ If you don't know where you're going, you won't get there. It makes sense, therefore, to set goals for yourself and your business. They needn't be long-winded, but they do need to be realistic. The gurus recommend you establish goals for 1 year, 3 years, 5, 10 and 20. Hard to project out that far, but there's nothing wrong with dreaming! Statistics show that those people who set goals are better organized, have more of a purpose and usually achieve what they set out to do.

- ❑ Setting goals will also help you measure your achievements and progress. But don't set yourself up. Just be easy the first time 'round. Maybe your business goals might include
  - spending at least 4 (preferably 8) hours a week on marketing. (Don't forget that taking someone to lunch, making notes about what needs to be done for your business card, making a phone call to a lead are part of that time spent!)
  - develop a simple marketing plan for some aspect of your business.
  - getting one new customer every 2 months
  - organizing your paperwork to flow easier
  - join one active, meaningful committee
  - setting 1 year, 3 year, 5, 10 and 20 year goals.

- ❑ Break down your marketing plan into small, easy-to-do bits, and make a schedule for tackling them. One a day. One a week. One a month. Doesn't matter how frequent, just make sure you do it consistently. One step at a time.

Marketing Plan (continued)

- ❑ Who are your potential customers? It's not such a tough question to answer, if you think about it. Here's how you can easily find out. Pull out all your records of customers past and present. Make a chart of where they live, what their income is, how old they are, what you've done for them, and any other pertinent information that will help you build a profile of *your* typical customer.

- ❑ Write down the type of organizations and people who have hired you for consulting assignments in the past. Do this for each of your market segments, including those you want but currently do not have.

- ❑ Include the following for each type of organization you serve: number of people, annual revenues, expected growth, industry, buying cycles, and buying policies. Also include information about contacts such as: personal characteristics, interests/hobbies, management styles, methods for finding consultants, and buying/hiring considerations. How can you let your prospects know you are in business?

- ❑ Make decisions based on the market's needs, NOT your needs or your company's needs.

- ❑ Look for that need among unfilled wants, disadvantages in established services and products, gaps in otherwise well-served markets, and more economical ways of satisfying expensively met requirements.

- ❑ Look for barriers or blockages re: innovation & what you want to achieve but can't because of some apparently immovable barrier - then go over or around it.

"Go back!"

- ❑ Test marketing includes focus groups, direct mail surveys, and telemarketing, and "is an invaluable tool that minimizes busi-

Marketing Plan (continued)

ness risk. The information you uncover helps you target market segments, determine price, and develop promotional strategies."

- ❑ Developing a database (computer list) of your potential customers can be extremely time-consuming. One way to kick-start the process is to call a list broker (see the Yellow Pages), and order a list based on a number of "sorts". Ask them, for instance, to match your potential customer profile by developing a list of all the single parents between 25 and 50, and who are living with one child under 15 in zip code areas 03301-03309, and who have a household income between $55,000 and $75,000, and who drive a car. For online list brokers, see
<http://www.LookupUSA.com>

- ❑ Use this 3-step, test marketing plan to help you reach prospects with direct marketing:

  1. Identify prospects. Phone books, CD phone directories, subscriber lists from trade pubs, association newsletters, business directories;

  2. Create a compelling presentation: Direct marketing guideline: response is driven 40% by the prospect, 40% by the product, 20% by the presentation;

  3. Have something to deliver, like a prototype so you can act as though it almost exists.

My calls came from:
#1. Globe Advertising
#2. Web page
#3. Web page
#4. Referral from Frank

- ❑ To begin tracking the success of your referral/marketing network, institute a check sheet that tracks the origin of your calls. If it's a potential customer, ask the caller "May I ask how you heard of my service/product?" If it's a referral, note the source. Use this tracking system to focus your marketing efforts.

MiniPlans for the Image Component of Your Business

> "You never get a second chance to make a first impression"
>
> Head and Shoulders shampoo ad

This is a *great* line. It doesn't *matter* whether it sold shampoo. What's important is the message. It really *is* true. You don't *ever* have another chance to make a first impression on someone, which is why it's *so* important to figure out -- right from the beginning -- the best way to create the image you want people to know.

Random House defines image as "A mental representation of something previously perceived. A general or public perception." Those of you already in business may have difficulty changing the image people have of you, but with careful planning and work it can be done. Those of you just starting obviously have the best chance of creating the image you want. Regardless, right now is the time to start thinking about who you are, how you want people to think about you as a person/vendor, and how you want them to think about your services and products. Exactly what kind of image/impression do they need that will convince them to buy what you offer?

I put this discussion of the "image" component of your business right up front, because that's *really* what marketing is about, and it underlies every marketing decision you make about each of the components thereafter.

Your Identity and Your Image

There is much discussion in marketing circles about identity and image, and what the difference is between them.

To begin with, there should be *no* difference. The fact that people want to ascribe one gives some insight as to the reason why.

A *person*'s identity is something they acquire, something about which they have a choice, especially as they begin to mature. Their identity is their individuality, their unique personal nature. Although parts of their identity are theirs at birth, like their fingerprints, they develop their own personalities and other identifying characteristics along the way.

When a *company* is born, it has *no* identity and can never acquire one on its own. Its identity is one that it's owners consciously decide to give it. Unfortunately, because company owners pay little attention to them in the beginning, identities take on a nature which is many times calamitous. A company gets known for sloppy work, for instance, or for major shortcomings in service, and then finds it too hard to break away from its own stereotype.

At this point, image becomes an issue, because even though their work may be sloppy and they deliver poor service, they want their "image" to be different. But instead of taking time to correct the company's shortcomings, they spend lots of money trying to present a better (and probably false) image of the company which, in the end, causes even more problems. New customers believe the image, start doing business with the company, and are then bitterly disappointed when they meet the company's true identity.

So, back to the beginning. There really should be *no* difference between identity and image. If they're in congruence, the chances for your quick success are improved immeasurably.

What follows immediately is an outline that will help you define your identity. What follows that is a thorough discussion of image and how you go about managing it.

4-Step Process
for Determining Your Identity

1 Analyze your business's structure, strengths, distinguishing characteristics, benefits, and what sets your it apart. What are the "defensible differences?" How would you answer the question: "What makes you different from your competitor?"

Note:
Never try selling the actual product/service. Only sell what it does for the customer (its benefits), because that's all they really want to know.

(See: The Benefits Wheels elsewhere in this book.)

2 "The sound bite." ***Verbally articulate the benefits*** through a mission or vision statement, slogans, tag lines, monikers, company name, or other.

Here's a simple example of how to tighten up an existing mission statement:

Formerly:

The New Hampshire Alliance for Arts Education (NHAAE) is a non-profit organization dedicated to the support of partnerships, practices, and policies that make the arts a fundamental part of education in New Hampshire.

The ~~New Hampshire~~ Alliance for Arts Education ~~(NHAAE)~~ is ~~a non-profit organization~~ dedicated to ~~the support of partnerships, practices, and policies that~~ making the arts ~~a~~ fundamental ~~part of~~ to ~~education~~ learning ~~in New Hampshire~~.

Now:

The Alliance for Arts Education is dedicated to making the arts fundamental to learning.

Questions:

- Why/How do we do that?
- How will the "customer" benefit?
- How can we explain and show the benefits?

3 "The picture bite." ***Visually express the benefits*** through logos, symbols, monograms, colors, shapes, package designs. A word picture in an eye blink.

4 Develop strategies using all the above to leverage a competitive position.

Your Image (continued)

The proper imaging of yourself and your business is crucial and very complicated. You might want to again review "The Brand Called You" in Part 1.

If you never speak with, see, or write anyone, you won't have an image to worry about. But as soon as you peek out from under the covers in the morning, open your mouth, send someone a note, or give them something with your name on it, your image is exposed and working for you.

Keep in mind the definition of image:

> "A physical likeness, representation, or likeness of a person, photographed, sculpted, painted, or otherwise made visible. A mental representation of something previously perceived. A general or public perception; to picture in the mind; to imagine; to symbolize or typify." (Random House)

"Hey! It's me! What a great image!"

Because you can't be everywhere at once, or can't be there all the time, you need to plant images of yourself and your business in people's minds. However, whatever image you choose to give people is the one they'll remember, so choose carefully!

Unfortunately you don't have control over some of your images. If someone tells someone *else* about you, the second person has a reflection of your image which may not be totally accurate or desirable. Then again, it could also be better, maybe even too good, so person #2 has unrealistic expectations about the way you look (the old blind date trick), or how you talk, or what your services provide, or what your product can do.

Another imaging device over which you have little control is your body language. Between 65% and 85% of face-to-face communication takes place without you ever opening your mouth. The *way* you stare, smell, breathe, walk, dress, tilt your head, blink your eyes, fold your arms, distribute the weight on your feet, make hand gestures, nod your head, twitch, or show fear, interest, empathy, happiness, sadness, boredom, or impatience

Your Image (continued)

all convey the most honest image of you anyone will ever get. You may not want them to have it, but they'll get it anyway.

You can't see yourself, so what's the Best Advice? Make sure what you're thinking, feeling, and saying are all in congruence! You can't have a running dialogue in your head about how unappreciative someone is for not understanding what you're telling them and expect it not to show outwardly in some way. In this particular instance, if this "unappreciative" person's business is important to you, you need to find some way to overcome your impatience so you don't turn away dollars.

Maybe you need to find out more about why this person doesn't understand. Are you speaking too fast or unclearly? Have you overlooked some key information? Have you properly diagnosed the other person's "wants" and accurately concluded that your service or product can help? Have you tried empathizing with the other person's resistance?

But even if this particular person's business is *not* important to you, in one way or another, they *will* pass on your image to someone else, and that *next* person may be someone important to you.

Luckily, the following are images of you over which you *do* have control:

- knowledge of your business and your products/services
- the identity of your business/service/product
- description of your services/products
- flyers about your products/services
- the way your office looks
- the way your associates look, act, and talk
- news releases
- your letterhead
- what you write on your letterhead
- your
    - business envelope
    - invoice format and message
    - advertising messages
    - public relations activities
    - business card (paper color, ink color, information, moniker)
    - phone message
- and many others

The sheer number of these makes it imperative that you seek professional advice to help define both your image and your imaging materials so they all work together toward a common end.

Let's take a look at what can be done with some of them.

One More Thing!

Printed materials are the most common items people use to represent themselves. Printed materials consist of two parts: the visual and the verbal, and despite what you think, the visual is far more important.

If the material (brochure, flyer, business card, etc.) is not visually appealing, people won't be drawn to it and may never even get to the verbal/written part, regardless of how well it's written!

Lots of factors contribute to whether something is visually appealing, even the "block" of text. If the paragraphs are not indented, for instance, your eye will have a hard time finding the first sentences and may not even try.

If the lines are too widely spaced apart, your eye knows it won't be able to hold the sentences together and may therefore just skip over the material. Or if the text is "justified," meaning the right and left sides of the paragraph are straight up and down, the spacing between the words or letters may be varied which might be distracting.

If the photos are poor quality, or not clear, or don't add to the "story," or if there isn't enough white space to provide relief throughout, you'll avoid the piece altogether.

If the colors for the paper (the "stock"), or the text or the headlines aren't compatible, are too light, or aren't strong enough, your eye will not be engaged and won't let your mind be engaged either.

Once again let me say that the visual appeal of whatever it is that represents you is very, very important.

Just to make the point crystal clear.

Suppose you wanted to buy a new car and you found the exact one you wanted: the right model, handled well, comfortable seats, awesome sound system, fast -- essentially it was your dream car.........but it was an ugly mustard green with orange stripes all over it.

Would you bother buying it? Or would you wait for something else?

Even though this was your dream car, you'd probably not bother with it.

So. Visual appeal is very important, and can make or break a relationship with a potential customer.

This is one more reason to take a deep breath and realize that you probably shouldn't design the material yourself but should instead hire someone who has the expertise.

Your Image (continued)

❑ Here's a difficult Mini-Marketing© concept, but it's one of the most important in this book!

You should *never* try selling the actual product or service. You should only sell what it does for your customer, because that's all your customer really wants to know. This is an important distinction, and it'll pay you to understand the diffference.

Furthermore, when the customer actually buys a product or service, they're not *really* buying it. They're buying what they think it'll *do* for them, its "benefits." (Look again at "Figuring Out the Benefits" in Part 1.)

Let me argue first for the concept, then address the obvious ramifications it has for marketing your business.

> *"You should never try selling the actual product or service. You should only sell what it does for your customer, because that's all your customer really wants to know."*
>
> ron king

Whhaaat?

Suppose you go to a superstore, you're walking down the aisle, and you see a shelf full of "Soothums." You have no idea what they are but you're intrigued by how they look, so you stop. Would you just pick one up, take it to the register, and go home? Probably not. So if I'm the person who made these "Soothums," and I've spent my entire marketing budget trying to get you to do just that, I've wasted my money. I forgot I have to tell you what this Soothum does, and how it's going to help you get something done, or done easier, or faster, or cheaper, or without as much hassle, or with less odor, or with more enjoyment, or...

I should instead have spent my entire budget convincing you

of the benefits of my product. Because if I do a good job showing you how “Soothum” will positvely impact your life, and if I can get you to imagine what it would be like to have one in your life or how much better your (life, job, kids) would be if you had this thing in your possession, I don’t even need to mention the actual product. If you can be convinced by what I say, you’ll buy the Soothum, and you’ll buy it without even having tried it!

Same idea for those of you selling services. You’re selling what the service will *do* for the customer, how it will help them solve a problem, make their lives easier, be better managers, resolve personal issues, or work more efficiently.

So. Back to what I said in the beginning: “When you’re selling something, your objective is not to sell the actual product or service. Your objective is to sell what that product or service will do for your customer.”

Now, ipso facto, the second part also makes sense: “When the customer actually buys a product or service, they’re buying what they think it’ll *do* for them They’re buying its benefits.”

Enough said? Enough said.

How’s this relate to your marketing? The first thing is to make sure that when you develop a product or service, it meets a prospective customer’s want/need (real or perceived). The narrower the gap between the product/service and its ability to solve a customer’s problem, or meet a customer’s want/need, the higher the value of the product/service, and the higher the liklihood of a sale.

Problem/want/need + product/service = problem solution, happiness, value

Your Image (continued)

Or, in other words, the closer the product/service comes to accuately and completely solving a problem or meeting a need, the higher its value and the more the customer will be willing to pay for it.

Therefore, when you put together your marketing plan, your entire emphasis needs to be focused on how the product or service meets that need.

- ❑ Now here's a great way to use the internet (if you have access to it). Check out **<http://www.iprint.com>** which offers a complete, fully automated, self-service for creating and ordering commercial printing. It offers elements of design, desktop publishing, electronic order-processing, and commercial printing in an interactive format to deliver personalized and customized business cards, letterhead, labels, and business forms. Once you're happy with your designs, they're transmitted to local printers to obtain lowest cost estimates, and the job is printed and delivered within seven working days thereafter! (Info from the Boston Journal 4/11/97)

- ❑ One of the exercises I offer my workshop participants helps put into perspective the difference between talking about yourself and someone else. When you're with a group of strangers, and you're asked to "go around the table, introduce yourself or your business," don't you usually get just a wee bit anxious as it gets closer to your turn? Well, it seems to happen to most everyone, so maybe it's normal.

  In my groups, after I announce that's what we're going to do, invariably I see some people stiffen up a little, some people groan, and most people shift in their seats. So we talk about these reactions, and try to find out what's going through people's minds, and then I say "Instead of introducing yourselves, I'd like you to find out about the person next to you and then introduce them."

Your Image (continued)

For some reason, it's a whole lot easier. We'd rather talk about someone else than about ourselves. One of the reasons is that we know too much about ourselves, so it's hard to know what to share, how much of it is important, and how much hidden stuff (that we may not want others to know about) is coming across with our tone of voice or body language.

When you talk about someone else, you know only what they've told you, and you really don't have a stake in whether you convey it accurately. Recommendation? Here are a number of ways to begin your own introduction:

> "People tell me I'm very good at...."
> "I've put together several unique concepts that allow me to offer my clients the best financial planning (or whatever)..."
> "While I was in college, I recognized a need for 24 hour copying services, so I..."
> "People always told me I should sell the toy I made my son, so I..."
> "I really like helping people through crises, so it seemed natural that I should..."

And so on. What I recommend is that you come up with something and then practice, practice, practice it (in front of your mirror first, then in front of best friends, then good friends, then OK people, then strangers).

After all, this is you marketing yourself, so the better and clearer you convey your image, the better the possibility of business down the road.

please continue ➡

Your Image (continued)

- ❑ If your office has a receptionist, make sure they are *extremely* friendly and *very* customer-service oriented. Train them to take information, ask questions, and handle difficult situations, then monitor them *frequently*. They are *your* image, both in face-to-face situations and over the phone. *Do not let this one slide.*

- ❑ The clearer you are about what you do, the easier it is to be excited about it, to find the best people to share it with, and to find the best *ways* to share it (the marketing strategies). Find a way to explain what you do in enough detail so the layperson understands exactly the nature of your service, why it's important to them, and why they should consider doing business with you. Your verbal explanation should take no more than 10-15 seconds, the usual amount of time you have someone's attention after they say "So, what do you do for work?"

- ❑ Make sure your image conforms to the way you'd like people to think about your service. If they are looking for you to help them organize their thoughts, but your office is always a mess, they might think you can't help them. If one of your good referral sources dresses rather formally, they may not be able to get around the very casual way you dress, which may affect their confidence in your ability to help the people they refer.

"My image is pretty clear, isn't it? You can tell I'm just a happy-go-lucky guy!"

- ❑ Look at your office with fresh eyes (or have a trusted friend give you a critique). Are there changes you could make that would make it friendlier, more comfortable, brighter, fresher, warmer, neater, handicapped accessible?

- ❑ Identify at least three organizations that cater to your prospective customer base. Join those organizations. More importantly, attend their meetings as a way of showing yourself, collecting other people's names and cards, and extending your network. Follow-up on the contacts by using a good contact management program (see the Technology Section)!!!

Your Image (continued)

❑ The Office

I am well aware that many people in business today do not have offices. Or, if they do, the converted basement, spare bedroom, family room, or kitchen table would not be welcome places for customers to visit. Nevertheless, many of your customers may still wonder whether you are a reliable purveyor if you don't show them some bricks and mortar. For them, it may be a sign of stability, and they may have trouble identifying and doing business with you if you can't at least make the offer of showing them your facilities.

If you have a presentable office or facility that creates the kind of image you want, show it off. Or, if you're looking to refresh your image, and you recently moved or remodeled, it's a great excuse for an open house. Even if only 8 people come, it's 8 more people that know where you are and what you do.

These days it's less likely that a consultant or owner of a small service business has a fancy office, storefront, or manufacturing plant. They have "virtual offices" and/or "mobile offices," two modus operandi that are beginning to be fairly widely accepted, thank goodness. Though the service provider or consultant has intellectual property which does not need a place to "be," per se, it does need to be packaged well so that it conveys an image of standing alone, appearing stabile, and looking like it has good value.

This is why imaging materials are critical.

My Office

Your Image (continued)

- [ ] Design a **flyer or brochure** that more accurately reflects what you do or some new service you're trying to promote. Then come up with a comfortable way to send it to the people who would like to know about what you offer.

  There are several main sections you should include (or consider including) in your brochure/flyer, and several design elements:

  - the name of your business (if you have one. If you don't, you can use your name) together with an epithet (a characterizing phrase) for your business/yourself;
  - a clear, concise statement about the benefits of your business;
  - the categories of clients you wish to serve;
  - years of experience;
  - your photo, so people can see who they're dealing with;
  - why your services are able to fulfill your customer's needs:

    Talk to existing clients. Find out what they like about: • you • your style • coming to you.
  - your approach/attitude toward the service you're providing;
  - your training;
  - credentials/qualifications for yourself, your staff and/or your associates (if you have them);
  - testimonials from satisfied customers/referral sources;
  - memberships in trade, professional or other organizations;
  - your facilities, especially if something about it might help you win customers (great parking, comfortable atmosphere, private entrance);
  - address, phone, fax, email, internet (web page) address;
  - attractive font (style of individual letters in the alphabet);
  - attractive plastic, wood, or paper. (There are several companies that sell pre-designed paper. You can use it if you don't want a unique look, but you do run the risk of

choosing a paper that another business in your community may also be using);

- logo. If you don't have one but want one, a graphic designer, desktop publisher, arty friend, or someone else can easily design a logo using your name and a piece of free clip art. Say your name is Smith and you loan money for vacations;

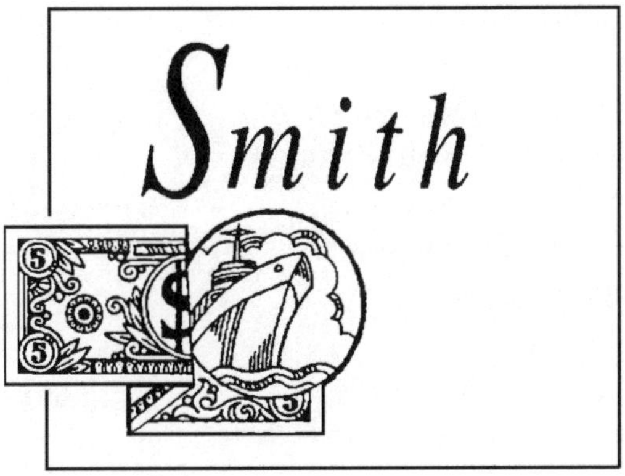

- other graphics, which could be artfully designed letters in the alphabet, clip art, photos, or drawings;
- colored paper and/or ink (other than, or in addition to black). Studies show that *ads* always attract more attention if color is added. The same applies to brochures, but for different reasons. Brochures are generally not in side-by-side competition, although that does occur. A brochure needs to be attractive in its own right, because the more memorable it is, the easier it is to remember the message -- or to go back and read it again;
- white space, white space, white space;
- attractive packaging. (In what will you send your brochure? Or will it be a self-mailer?);
- attractive design. Work with a designer to pull together all the above elements in a balanced design, especially if you don't have an artistic eye and/or don't know how to work with printers.

Your Image (continued)

❑ If you can't afford a brochure/flyer at this time, go ahead and develop your idea about your product/service anyway, prepare an executive summary, set it up nicely on your letterhead, and send it out to a targeted group meeting your customer profile.

❑ Design a new **business card**, a process which could drive you crazy. There are so many choices of materials, colors, and information, that unless you either know exactly what you want or are working with someone who can help you make decisions, you *will* go crazy.

Keep in mind that your business card is one of the most important imaging pieces you'll have. They're a convenient way to exchange information, and can provide the backup or reminder needed once you reach a certain point in your negotiation or conversation. You will always run into people who say "I'll send information. What's your address?" or who will ask you outright for your business card.

In the business world, the card is a form of currency, and if people find it valuable enough for its information or it's beauty (hopefully both), they'll hang onto it. My card is a mini-brochure. It's a fold-over, and it's practically the only imaging piece I ever use. It's printed with gold ink on expensive paper and has the look and feel I really wanted, so I'm really proud when I hand it out.

One of my workshop participants said she practiced "differentiated" marketing, which to her meant slightly changing her message depending on the audience she was addressing. She was able to tailor her services to meet specific needs, so I recommended she develop more than one business card. The look of each card should be consistent so her image wouldn't be compromised (that is, she might want to use the same paper stock for each, the same ink, logo, epithet, or what-have-you), but the message about her services/products could be slightly changed.

To get started, look in the yellow pages for printers. Many of them will not print cards in their own shops but will send them out to specialty companies. But your printer will have demo books with hundreds of business card samples you can look at, and you'll get lots of ideas just from looking. Basic cards are fairly inexpensive. Once you start adding lines of information, graphics, ink colors, or photos, they can get really expensive. At that point, you'll probably be better off going to a local printer who will produce your card from scratch.

See next page for design details. ➡

❑ Business card design details

Business cards can take many forms:

- standard and non-standard one-sided,
- standard and non-standard 2-sided,
- bi-fold and tri-fold, folded to standard and non-standard sizes,
- infocards, with many standard and non-standard sized "pages" glued at one end,
- Rollodex cards.

They may contain basic information -- and then some:

- name
- epithet
- PO Box or address, city, state, full zip. (If you ever expect overnight mail deliveries, you need a street address.)
- phone, fax, (email and web page addresses, if you have them)
- what you do
- how you do it
- categories of client services
- your photograph
- a logo
- testimonials

Materials:

- You can have business cards made of paper (dull or shiny), plastic, wood, metal, cloth, or anything else that reflects who you are and what you do. To look and feel substantial enough to make and leave a good impression, use material that is equivalent to "80 pound paper cover stock."
- Colors: of the paper used (the "card stock," usually 80#) and for the ink. Words can be printed with flat or raised letters and with different colored inks, including silver, bronze and gold. You can also ask that your words be gold or silver embossed.

> Keep in mind that the business card, the brochure, and the cover letter are you!
>
> You therefore need to think how you want yourself represented. If your brochure or business card looks unattractive, your practice will appear unattractive. If they appear cheap, your practice will appear cheap. If they're sloppy, people will think you and the way you conduct business are sloppy.
>
> There may be some people who are not bothered by what they see, and there may be some who like sloppy, cheap, unattractive-looking brochures and business cards. But as they will be in a minority, please don't let these representations of you be designed with those people in mind!

- ❑ Your sign. If you have one, take a good look at it, and remember it's out here giving off a signal day and night for all to see. There are lots of potential customers who'll use the condition of your images (sign, office, materials) as a way of determining the kind of service they're going to get, so your sign better look good and be in great condition. I can't tell you how many I see that are crooked, peeled, and illegible from the weathering.

Your Image (continued)

❑ Newsletters are a great way to stay in touch with your customers. Everyone's doing them, so some of their impact is lost, but if you make them attractive and useful, there's a better chance they'll be read.

Keep in mind that the main idea is to keep your name, picture and the benefits of your services/products in front of people all the time so when the time comes for them to buy, they'll make the decision in your favor.

*"I've got some **great news** to help you out!"*

If you have graphic software or a more advanced word processing program, you might be able to design your own newsletter. Or, you can hire someone to develop a newsletter template for you.

Naturally, the writing should be up to you.

Some design guidelines:

- Develop a template that remains the same for each issue. A template is the framework for every graphic and text item that appears in the newsletter. It essentially dictates the positioning of each item so the newsletter has a consistent look and feel about it.
- If you can afford it (about $40 dollars extra) try using another color in addition to black. Color has been proved to be an attention-getter.
- Use lots of white space to balance off other visual elements.
- Develop a memorable name for your newsletter.
- Use descriptive headlines.
- Keep stories short, sweet, and meaty.
- Include your photo and list of services/products.
- Make sure to include name, address, phone, email, and Web page address of business.
- If you use an epithet, include it.

MiniPlans for the Customer Service Component of Your Business

I don't have to tell you that servicing your customers is of paramount importance. Without customers, you *have* no business, so giving them extraordinary or exceptional service is the number one way to keep them coming back and referring you time and again. Customer service can not be a sometime thing. Every aspect of your business has to exude an interest in and attentiveness to your customer. Taking an extra step, giving more value, following-up, responding politely, smiling, resolving problems quickly and in the customers best interest, designing foolproof responses for you and your staff that always place the customer ahead of any other considerations.... are mandatory. Someone once said "A customer is someone who has yet to find a better alternative."

"Yes, My Customer"

Listen to this new organizational management idea: now the thinking is that if you want the *customer* treated well, management has to treat the *employee* well, so actually the *employee* comes first, *not* the customer. If employees are happy on every level, feel unequivocal support from you and the rest of management, and are given what it takes to feel the pride of ownership in their organization, they'll become such unbelievable customer service advocates, you'll hardly need a policy.

Here's another finding. A.T. Kearny Financial Institutions Group says that a "consistent, customer-focused marketing strategy can double a financial institution's profitably." Based on my own research and findings, it'll do the same for you. When you're thinking about a "customer focused marketing plan," keep in mind that at different stages, customers need and want different things.

You wouldn't, for instance, greet the tire-kicking customer the same way you would a customer who has continued to do business with you for the past three years. The existing customer expects to be acknowledged, revered, appreciated, recognized. They may even expect you to know something about their personal life, or the groups to which they belong (like the Chamber of Commerce). They're looking for special treatment.

Remember I said that at different stages a customer may want or need different things? It's more than just the personal things. If you *really* want to keep their business, you need to know something about *their* customers, or *their* business.

They expect you to remember what they bought and what they still need. If your business is printing, they would love it if you called them 2-3 months before they normally put out their year-end calendar or report, or before their big trade show where they'll need flyers for new products they're offering. Or if you're a web page consultant, they'd love it if you made a proposal to help them get their new products on their web page.

Anticipating customer's needs before they do is one sign of an outstanding provider of services or products, and one that really wants to keep the customers they have. That, and delivering more than you promise.

Now. One last thing. I ran across this a few months ago, and I don't know where it came from. Even if the calculations are a little off, the point is unmistakable:

If 99.9% were good enough:

Every year there would be 15,000 newborn babies dropped during delivery,

Every week there would be 500 incorrect surgical procedures performed;

Every day there would be 2 unsafe landings at O'Hare, and

Every hour there would be 2,000 checks deducted from the wrong bank account, and 16,000 pieces of mail lost by the US Postal Service!

❑ If you're in a highly competitive business, you'll frequently be a position where a potential customer will either give hints that they're "kicking the tires and comparing prices" or verbally threaten to go to a competition. In either case you're in a *wonderful* position to do some further marketing of your own service/product. For example:

• Take the initiative and recommend a competitor you know who will treat them right. You could even call the competitor, identify yourself, and tell them you have someone in your office who's looking for a product/service, and you wondered whether your competitor could help. If you don't call, tell the customer to mention your name when they go see competitor John. There's lots of gain in doing any of this. First, it's great PR. You'll become known as someone who's looking out for your fellow businesspeople, you're supporting local businesses, you're not greedy and therefore more trustworthy; you become a great resource that customers will learn to rely on and trust, which eventually brings you more business, etc., etc.

• You will come across as an expert to the potential customer if you provide them with a checklist of the benefits they would get if they were *your* customer. The potential customer will then have this list in mind when shopping around, and if you've done your homework well, and have displayed it nicely in the checklist, your competitors won't come *close* to beating you out on the combination of price, service, and quality.

❑ Make sure you return phone calls! There is nothing more rude or inconsiderate than making someone call more than once, or maybe twice, to speak with you. Make it a rule to get back to people within 24 hours. Your business depends on customers or potential customers being able to trust you, have confidence in you and your business, feel like they're being taken care of. If you don't care enough to call them back, they won't care enough to be your customers.

❑ Answering the phone soon after it rings has become a benchmark customer service item for many companies. Because life moves so fast these days, customers get frustrated if the phone rings more than 4 times and they'll usually hang up. This is no good for sales, image, or confidence in your business.

❑ Returning phone calls from the press is a must. If you've worked hard to create the impression that you're an expert in your field, or have special knowledge about a process or item, the press may be calling for clarification on a question about a related issue. It's great advertising for you.

❑ A live person in your office, a live answering service, a voice mail system, an answering machine, in that order, if you have to make a choice about how your business phone gets answered. Not having any one of these is inexcusable.

- While we're on the business of answering machines: for heaven's sake, get one that sounds good. There is nothing worse for your business image than a tinny, poor quality, unprofessional-sounding, white-noisy machine. Check it out before you buy (or make sure you can bring it back). Then write and practice a script before you record your message. If you can't make it sound enticing and friendly, have someone else record it for you.

- AND get a machine that allows you more than 2 seconds for your message or the caller's message. From experience, you know how frustrating and embarrassing it is to have the line go dead on you if you're calling a business to make an appointment, or explain a problem, or just leave your name, address, and phone. Talk about lost revenues!

❑ Under promise and over deliver! And you'll look like a hero every time, which gives your customer confidence in you, which makes them want to use you again and refer you to others.

❑ If you can't afford a newsletter to maintain a presence with your customers, try sending postcards, preferably with a unique design. On the front: photo and quote; on the back: brief description of product/service/presentation, plus phone number. No bulk mail available for postcards, but they're cheaper to mail than first class, even at bulk rate.

❑ LISTEN to your customers. If you're so convinced your product/service will solve your customer's problems, despite what they say to the contrary, *there's every chance you'll blow the relationship and lose the sale.*

Why? Because you'll be anxious to convince the customer of everything at once. But keep in mind the customer needs to come at it slowly. Think of how you feel when you're being hussled. It's not that the "hussler" doesn't know what they're talking about. They probably know all too well. So they answer *all* your questions, and have *all* the answers, and want to convince you *way* too eagerly. So you get suspicious and shut down. You don't have time to process, to sort out exactly what questions you have, or how the product/service is going to affect the way you've *always* done things before.

Place yourself in your customer's shoes, and recognize that LISTENING to them is a real gift which will probably bring you the sale. Listening will allow you to actually *understand* what the customer needs and *why* they think they need it. By gently probing with questions about their needs, and then listening to the answers, you can easily tailor your responses, demonstrations, handouts, models, services, products, or whathaveyou so the customer feels like they're getting *exactly* what they need.

What if you're not the listening kind? Either prepare to lose lots of sales, eat lots of crow, work extra hard to get (and keep) customers -- or **learn to listen**. There are courses on communication which include "active listening," or if you don't need a lot of convincing, pick up a self-help book.

Make sure this "Listening to the Customer" policy is understood by everyone in your organization including the person who answers the phone. "Huh? Whadyousay?" or cutting people off to put them on hold, or not trying to figure out first exactly where to route their call, is not listening!

❑ Finding a way to get customer feedback is very important, because you need to have a reality check. You may think you're doing a great job, but your customers may think otherwise, so you need to ask them. One of the easiest ways is by way of a questionnaire, which can be long or short.

After a product is sold or a service provided, send out a letter with a stamped postcard within on which are a few simple questions requiring yes/no answers, such as : Were you happy with our service? Did the product/service meet your expectations?

As you can easily change the questions, try varying them depending on what you'd like to know about your business from the customers' perspectives. So you could ask about parking, or hours of operation, or quality of merchandise, or adequate signage.

Make sure to leave room for "Comments." This is where you'll get unsolicited information which, in many cases, is the most valuable of all.

You can ask people for their names, but make it optional. However, the customers who *do* give their names *as well as* information (or ask for another product/or service), should be attended to immediately!

MiniPlans for the Referrals Component of Your Business

❑ Take one of your referral sources to dinner each week. Discuss their business with them, and new/better ways you might be able to help them be even more successful. Ask them for referrals. There is one person I know whose only marketing consists of doggedly following this plan.

A therapist I know takes her hairdresser out to lunch on a regular basis to thank her for all the referrals!

❑ Ask your referral sources whether they'd like you to develop a new service. Are they frustrated because they like you and the way you work or what you offer , but can't use you enough because you don't offer the services/products they need? If this is the case, think carefully about what you can do, either to develop the service/product yourself, or to find an outstanding colleague to whom you can refer — and maybe with whom you can trade referrals.

❑ Try getting permission from your best referral sources to place your information card/brochure in their places of business. This accomplishes lots of things at once: you get yet another chance to visit with them and remind them about your services/products; because your brochures will get dirty, dog-eared, or depleted, you have reason to visit their place of business on a regular basis to check on and replace the brochures; if their business is a busy one, you get exposure to potential customers or other potential referral sources.

❑ If you know a competitor provides a service/product you don't, chances are you provide one they don't. Call them up. Go for coffee. Talk about ways you can both feel comfortable about sharing referrals with each other. Even if it's not a competitor, but you know the person could be a good referral source, is there anything you can offer to help them with? Can you put up a poster about their business? Can you volunteer to speak at their next business meeting if their group is looking for speakers?

❑ Find a way to give incentives to people who give you referrals.

❑ Get a letter of reference from a good referral source, and ask whether you can use it to show other potential referral sources you want to cultivate (you've done research and know who you want to target, right?). This would become part of your strategy for expanding your referral source network (part of your marketing plan).

❑ Much of your business should come from existing customers. It is OK, therefore, to think carefully how to cultivate this aspect of your referral network, so customer referrals will not only continue, but increase.

❑ The reason your customers refer other people to you is because you are serving them well. They trust you, they are happy with you, they feel comfortable in your presence, they like your product/service, they know you'll treat their friends the same way. Trust is the key word, here. When Jane recommends a restaurant, a movie, a REALTOR®, a dentist, the Daytimer, or some other service or product, she's putting herself and her judgment at risk, because her friends trust her. If the food is bad, the movie is lousy, and the REALTOR® bombs, Jane's credibility suffers in the eye of her friend, so Jane's going to be very cautious about making recommendations. You can therefore see why it's so important to do whatever needs to be done to help Jane feel and remain confident about you and your product/service.

❑ Because Jane won't risk her reputation, she'll be very careful about referring you. The easier you make it for her, the more information you give regarding the extent and quality of your services and products, the more comfortable she'll feel about handing out your literature, your cards, your name.

Referrals (continued)

❑ The easiest way to bring this up with your customer? "I thought I'd let you know that I'm beginning to focus my service in the area of ...... , for the main reason that.... so if you know anyone who wants.... I'd appreciate your telling them. I even have a new brochure if you want more information." (Give her brochures.)

❑ Or, if you feel comfortable with it, you could talk about your new service/product, and ask for the names of people she thinks might be interested. This works especially well if, say, your customer is closely connected with your previously identified target market.

❑ Confidentiality may be an issue. If you're talking to a new customer, the first step is to go back through him. You will probably ask John where he heard about you or your service/product (you should always do this. It helps you track your referral sources.) When John tells you, and it happens to be another customer, you can say "The next time you see Jane, *please* give her my sincerest thanks for referring you to me." That, in itself may be enough incentive for Jane to keep spreading the word. It also shows John how much you cherish the referral, which also gives him further incentive to spread the good word.

❑ If you can think of a good incentive for, say, a physician, or a meeting planner, or a training director, to keep sending you referrals, please let me know. I recommend treating them to dinner on occasion as a way of saying thanks. Or sending flowers to their office. Not for every new customer, of course, but for every second or third one. Or hand delivering a gift certificate from their favorite bookstore, or movie theatre, or music store, with a handwritten note. Some marketing consultants specialize in ways that sometimes get people's attention (sending crazy things like big erasers, big aspirins, or huge post-it notes).

❑ Whenever anyone does anything for your your business, send them a nice, handwritten thank you note on a distinctive card.

Referrals (continued)

Confidentiality is sometimes an issue with referrals, but a card (*Don't type it. Handwrite it)* saying "Thanks for all your support;" and/or "the growth of my business depends on people like you;" and/or "I'm extremely appreciative of the confidence you continue to have in my services/products. Thanks so much for all your help." For a selection from over 200 unique business thank you messages on beautiful note cards, see **<http://www.minimarketing.com>**

> *Dear Jane,*
>
> *Thanks for helping my business grow.*
>
> *Best, Ron*

❑ But people will do other things, as well. Someone might recommend that you speak at the next Chamber meeting. Or someone might recommend you serve on a special committee or Board. Or someone might send you a notice about a seminar in which you have interest.

❑ Refer people constantly if you can't service them yourself. This does several things. One, it shows you're helpful and open about the competition which promotes a good feeling a sense of trust and a good sense of community. People are going to seek out the information anyway, so this gives you a chance to show your good side. But also, you're in a position to find out what customers *really* need (so you can properly guide them). This will also give you a second chance to ascertain exactly what they need -- and you might find out that you can help them after all. If you keep hearing the same request over and over again, and you feel comfortable with the idea of expanding your services to include that one as well, do it! and keep the business for yourself!

❑ Bend over backwards to add value to your services so your clients will report good things back to the person who referred them.

❑ Make absolutely sure you're on time for appointments.

❑ Make a point to know about a customer's interests; send relevant articles or notes. This budding relationship will generate referrals

Referrals (continued)

❑ Offer to collaborate so the referral source will get to know you better and feel more comfortable referring to you.

❑ Give them a reason to tell someone (a potential customer or another referral source) about your business.

❑ Do *whatever* is necessary to encourage word of mouth. Think what you can do that will be so amazing, so nice, so wonderful, so thoughtful, so memorable, that they'll tell a friend or someone else who could send you referrals.

My printer, who also offers internet and telephone access, bends over backwards to give me outstanding service. As a result, I tell everyone about him. Here's his email: aweiss@abovediscount.com. He providses service worldwide.

❑ Develop materials or a system that would make it easy for a referral source to convey information to *their* customers about *your* business (brochures, leaflets, posters...).

❑ Ask them for more referrals! Asking for business always generates more business, but the question is rarely asked.

❑ If you can set up your relationship with customers to accommodate the following, this idea can produce results. If you know a customer got more than they ever expected, ask them for five (more/less) referrals. If nothing is forthcoming within a reasonable time, send them humorous invoices and dunning notices. "You owe us 5 referrals. Number paid: 2. Still owed: 3" Just don't carry it too far, or you'll be harassing them.

❑ Ask for referrals! This is one of the easiest and best ways to get more business. The idea, of course, is that if your customers are happy with you, their friends might be, too. But if you don't ask, they don't know you have the time to service others. So ask. Even on the bottom of your invoices, hand write a note saying "Thanks again for your business. Referrals welcomed."

A Quickie Marketing Plan for Referrals

- Develop better referral sources
    - friends
    - past/current customers
    - other business owners (which?)
    - community groups (which?)
    - trade associations
    - other?
- by making them aware of my services and products and
- by encouraging and enhancing word-of-mouth opportunities through:

    1. targeted marketing to the above groups using:
        - printed materials.
        - personalized letters.
        - newsletters/single advertiser journals.
        - Other LC/NC technique.
        - visiting with referrals to review services.
    2. joining or volunteering services/giving away products to high profile groups;
    3. public relations activities (such as the following) directed to the above groups:
        - breakfast/lunch invitations.
        - workshops/informational meetings.
        - Chamber or other presentations from you, "the authority."
        - other low-cost/no-cost techniques.

MiniPlans for the "Keeping in Touch" Component of Your Business

- ❑ Customers have short memories, which is the best argument for keeping in touch with them. Using your imaging materials and office technologies (see those Sections in this book), devise strategies that will frequently put your name in front of your customers so they don't forget you.

  Some ideas:

  - Send postcards on a consistent basis (see discussion under the Service Section)
  - Send regular newsletters (see Imaging Section)
  - If you like the telephone, talk to your customers on a regular basis.
  - Invite your customers out to dinner occasionally.
  - Use a Contact Management/calendar program (see both the Technology and Office Procedures Sections) to remind you of customer's (and their family member's) birthdays, special events, or any other memorable occasions, so you can send them cards or notes, or call them.
  - Send faxes (see both the Technology and Electronic Media Sections).
  - Invite them to events/seminars/workshops that you schedule about your products/services.
  - Throw a party for them.
  - Periodically send/take them a little gift (nothing expensive) like a flower, plant, pen, letter opener, calendar, note pads (there are catalogues listing hundreds of these kinds of things).

MiniPlans for the PR/Advertising Component of Your Business

❑ Once marketing activities have a conscious place in your weekly schedule, allocate some time to joining a group that heightens awareness about you, either because you impress potential referral sources, or because potential customers get a firsthand glimpse of how you work.

❑ Even more straightforward might be to become a member of a board, regulating body, or committee.

❑ If you write well, write a letter to the editor. Doesn't have to be about something that appeared in the paper, but it must reflect something of general interest such as why you approach business the way you do, your responsibility to the community, or factors affecting your business. Such letters aren't great ideas unless you stick to a theme and write regularly.

❑ Also, try a guest column. Some of you live in small towns serviced by small papers always looking for material. They may be willing to take you on as a guest columnist to discuss topics having to do with a particular aspect of your business.

❑ Another, probably less available outlet for your prose is a trade journal. If you have ideas that can affect the industry, or research that can impact the way others conduct business, this is the stuff you should write about. The marketing effects on your business may not appear immediately, but three things happen: **1.** others begin seeing you as the expert, and will seek your advice; **2.** you can begin using reprints of the article(s) as part of your marketing campaign; **3.** you begin feeling like the expert with something to say that people want to hear.

❑ Here's a neat idea to get "news" coverage. Hire a freelance journalist to write an article about touting everything good about your company, then run it as an "advertorial in the paper. Use a reprint of it in a direct mailing.

❑ If you moved, developed a new service — or even if you felt like revamping your old services — put out a news release. "Jane Doe announces the introduction of a new service for families with ... (include all the essentials you can get away with, like details about the service, where you're located, telephone, your credentials, your areas of specialty). You'll need a good photo, so have one shot professionally. It will cost, but get several prints and use them whenever you can. (See the sample release later in this section.)

❑ Advertising: Keep in mind, advertising is an activity usually designed to appeal to a mass audience, and mass advertising is *very* expensive because you're paying to send your information out to a **mass**ive amount of people in the hopes that a small percentage will respond. It's better if you can figure out who those small numbers are, and target them with your information.

If, after doing the research, you think you *must* advertise (mass market) (and to be effective, you have to advertise frequently and consistently), make sure you pick the magazine, newspaper, newsletter, radio station, TV channel, yellow pages, or whatever medium, which *itself* targets the group which most fits the profile of your potential customer. You need to understand that that medium is taking your place in some respects. It is representing you and affecting your image. Here's how it works:

- I'm thinking of running an ad in a mass medium, possibly newspaper, radio, or TV. First I need to research the

PR/Advertising (continued)

demographics of their readership/listenership to make sure they are reaching my targeted group of potential customers, so I send for a press kit. I find that the Herald News has a significant readership of upscale, middle-aged businesspeople, and those are the people I'm trying to reach.

- I know from research done by the Marketing Council and other things I've read in this book (see "The Value of Consistency") that I have to advertise consistently and frequently to make it worthwhile, so I look at my budget and the rate sheet for the different size ads, and choose a size I can afford for the next 6 months.

- I contact the Herald, and I either ask for their help designing my ad (it's usually a free service, but their design skills may be limited), or I have a "camera ready" ad that either I designed or my graphics/marketing person designed. There are too many design factors to discuss here, but white space, a good headline, a demand feature ("Call..."), using key catch words, color, and some way to track the impact of the ad ("Ask for Jane"; or "Free bagel with this coupon") are all important.

- Due to my limited budget, the days I pick to run my ad each week or month are based on: statistics showing who reads the paper when, or special features being run by the paper, or whether information is time sensitive or based on something else happening in the community...

- Once the ad starts running, I track all calls/sales so I know whether my ad is working, which days "pull" better, etc.

PR/Advertising (continued)

❑ There's lots of discussion on whether to advertise on the radio. If you have a product to offer, maybe you should, especially if you know the radio station targets -- and is listened to by -- your potential clients. However, the value of radio advertising for services is not a sure bet at all. It's OK if you want to create an image, or keep your service in people's minds, but advertising on the radio rarely makes the phone ring.

❑ Be a guest on someone's talk show. The listening audience figures that the host must be picking top people as guests, so the guest therefore becomes an expert. If you are that "3rd party expert," there's a likelihood that new customers may call looking for your services.

❑ If you become a "3rd party expert," there's a good chance the media will call upon you more frequently to get a local spin on issues, which makes you sound even more like an expert, which means more people will call for your spin.... (Just make sure you're comfortable in front of a mike.)

❑ "Earned advertising:" Joining an association's Editor's Group (for instance the National Association of Real Estate Editors, **<http://www.naree.com>**) gets you in their source book as a writer and expert on certain topics. If the association properly markets their book to the right media people, you may be frequently called for your opinion and for quotes on the topic/issue.

❑ TV advertising is expensive, but here's a little gem from my friend Terry. If you're from the North country or hurricane prone areas where snow and winds abound, and school cancellations are frequent, make sure to let your local cable company know that your class, course, seminar, or other publicly offered event has been cancelled as well. These cancellations appear at the bottom of the screen for a good part of each of these mornings and give your business great exposure.

❑ This tip is last because it applies to all forms of advertising you decide to do: **Track it**! Track your advertising!

What you're trying to do is link the call/visit to whatever motivated the customer to make the decision to buy your product/service.

So if you placed an ad in the classified section of the *Local Herald* to run last Thursday, and someone called you Tuesday, it would be nice to know whether the call came as a result of the ad. If it did, but it's the only call that came in all week, whereas last week when you placed the same ad and ran it Friday and you got 20 calls the following week, what's that tell you?

Or if you decided to spend eight hours pinning your business card on every public bulletin board you could find, it would be nice to know if the time and expense paid off, wouldn't it?

So track your advertising. You can do this using one of several methods. If there's something special in your ad, like a unique phone number, or a code number people need to give you to get a special discount, or a coupon to be clipped, you clearly know -- without asking -- where the (new) customer heard about you.

If you've chosen a method to advertise like pinning up your business card and therefore don't have the option to include a tracking option, you need to get in the habit of asking people where they heard about you. And then *keep track of the information*!

Once you gather enough of it, you can make better decisions about where to spend your *next* advertising dollars.

PR/Advertising (continued)

Write a press release using the following format,
substituting your information where appropriate

****

(double-spaced, on letterhead)

For Immediate Release (this is a real one my wife sent out)

Contact: **Gerri King, Ph.D.**

603-224-2841 (NH)

800-789-5104 (US)

January 10, 2001—Dr. Gerri King from Concord, NH-based Human Dynamics Associates, Inc. (HDA) was awarded a contract by Anderson Consulting to work with world-wide staff around issues of conflict resolution and effective communication.

HDA will work with supervisors and managers at Andersen's Center for Professional Education in St. Charles, Illinois. The work will include classes, breakout sessions, and discussions with managers.

HDA provides facilitation and human relations consulting services to corporations, organizations and agencies throughout the United States, Canada, and Europe. For more information, contact Dr. Gerri King at HDA, 800-789-5104.

Send your release to the editors of your local metropolitan (and community) paper's business section, computer tabloids, business tabloids, and other local publications that are read by your target market. Sending an announcement about a local contract to a national publication won't get you very far. You can find the names and addresses of the right people by calling the publication or by looking on its masthead.

MiniPlans for the Office Procedures Component of Your Business

- ❑ Return calls as soon as humanly possible. It may mean that you become obsessive about checking in, and it may be that 90% of the time, no one will have called, but in the event someone does, and they need to speak with you right away (about a referral or about becoming a client of yours), you want to be there for them.

- ❑ Waiting in your waiting room can be lonely and intimidating for your clients, whether they be new or seasoned. Think of ways they might be made more comfortable. Do they have the kind of magazines they like? (Ask them!) Would they like coffee or tea? (An automatic coffee maker is cheap, the smell of coffee is friendly, disposable cups are cheap, and who knows? If you can find a blend of beans that's just right, people will look forward to coming to your office for more than one reason.) Should you dress up the office by painting it, cleaning it, or putting in more comfortable furniture? Do you have enough light to make your office bright and friendly? (Winter days can be real dark and dreary.)

- ❑ Check how your phone is being answered. If you have a service, or if you recorded a message yourself, what does it say? Have someone else listen to it and comment on how it makes them feel. Have someone else record the message if your can't. The voice and the message make up one of the images of you that people will carry around!

- ❑ **Contact Management.** Once you decide the exact people to whom you are sending or taking your marketing message, you need to keep track of the contacts you make with each of them. Such items as: what you promised them you'd do, what questions they asked (and what answers you gave them), how many brochures you dropped off and when you should check the supply again, when you need to call them again, what kind of business they have, how many referrals a year they send, what kind of thank you needs to be sent, their names, birthdays, addresses, phone numbers -- all need to be tracked. This is not easy unless you have a contact management program for your computer or a very good manual file and calendar system.

If you want to set up a manual system, try this. Use manila folders with end labels on which you write the customer's name. On the inside left, staple a lined sheet with 4 columns (date, time, contact person, subject of conversation). On the right hand side, prepare a form with the name of the person and/or company, addresses, phones, fax, email, directions to office, hours, receptionist's name, birthdates, etc. On the bottom should be a place to track the date and content of any mailings. Loose beneath the form are hard copies of all correspondence. Use both forms in conjunction with your calendar!

MiniPlans for the Electronic Communication Component of Your Business

- ❑ There are a lot of things happening on the Internet (the World Wide Web) these days, and everyone may be telling you that your business needs a "Web presence," but go slowly. Having America On Line (AOL) or another Internet Service Provider (ISP) "host" you web page is easy to line up, and not that expensive. *Creating* your Web page is another matter entirely.

  Web page creation is a whole business in itself and can be extremely costly, depending. You can hire someone to create it for you (the high cost varies depending on the page's complexity. While you might get away with $200-$500, large companies think nothing of spending 10's of thousands of dollars). Or you can learn to do it yourself. Creating Web pages requires knowing how to use HyperText Markup Language (HTML) for writing code that the Internet understands, tags, URLs, and a lot of other Internet protocols. Rather than torture yourself, use a page-authoring software program like PageMill from Adobe. They're supposed to be WYSIWHG (say "whyseewig" for "What You See Is What You Get") programs, but I've been trying to use PageMill for replicating some of the nicer pages I see on the Internet, and for the life of me, even after spending hours with the manual, I don't get it. A simple page, yes. But something a little complicated will take lots of your time.

  I digress. If you have a new, small business, you don't need a Web presence. Yet.

Electronic Communication (continued)

❑ However, if you've plowed ahead, and are really excited about trying to understand the Web, there are some sites that might help you get some simple-to-understand information. Check out **Web 101 (<http://hotwired.lycos.com/webmonkey/guides/>)** and go directly to "Get on the Web." Also, for basic aspects of web design, discussion groups about the net, and resource links, check: **<http://www.htmlhelp.com/>**.

❑ For free advice and tips on many things to do with small business, check **<http://www.sba.gov/>** A very comprehensive site from the US Small Business Administration. Information on starting a business, SBA loans, and other helpful services for business owners.

<http://www.sb.gov.bc.ca/smallbus/workshop/workshop.html> An on-Line Small Business Workshop. Very nice, simple, step-by-step advice on building a business. Presented by the British Columbia Provincial Government.

<http://www.eweekly.com/> Lots articles and advice related to sales, marketing, and advertising. Be cautious, because not all the advice here is good, but if you do decide to read articles, take a look at their past issues for plenty of helpful marketing ideas. Slow loading site.

❑ If you've already developed a Web page and want a way to check out what others experience when they pull it up on their computers, Web Site Garage is the place to go. Although you have to pay for many of their services, some are free. **<http://www.websitegarage.com>**

Or, if you want some practical tips for making your web site more efficient and effective, check out **<http://www.tlc-systems.com/webtips.shtml>**

Electronic Communication (continued)

❑ Email (electronic mail) can be very cost-effective for small businesses, whether you're selling products or services. Think of email as letters going back and forth via the phone between you and your customer. If you're a one-person show, and you frequently don't return to your office until after 5, email can be a lifesaver -- if you and your customers know each other's email addresses.

So the first hint is to make sure you always ask for the email address.

Then there are a couple of hints that might be helpful.

• There's something called the "signature" which you rarely, if ever, see, but which all your customers see. At the end of your message on their screen are several lines identifying the sender (you). Here's where your email address appears, the name of your company, maybe a slogan/epithet, and other information that will help the reader (your customer) recognize you and your company. Once you're in your email program, hunt around for the option/preference that allows you to change the "signature."

• Also, somewhere in the email software set-up, is a way you can put together groups ("batches") of email addresses so you can send the same email to a number of people (customers or otherwise). You can make up several groups which will allow you to customize several different messages.

• If you happen to belong to two internet service providers (ISPs) like I do (such as AOL and AT@T Broadband), and you get email at both addresses, you can ask one of them to forward email to the other. That way, you won't miss anything.

Electronic Communication (continued)

There is one drawback to email. Both of you need a computer, a modem, email software (that either stands alone or that is part of a service like AOL), and a phone line. If you do, and you both get used to using email, you can respond to your customers at 11 o'clock at night, if you want.

- ❑ Newsgroups. Chat Rooms, Discussion Groups. The Internet is full of hundreds of groups which meet on the computer to discuss specific topics. If you watch the discussion for a while, you may want to join in by responding to someone's question. Respond often enough, and the group may view you as an expert and send business your way.

- ❑ Faxing. Fax forward/fax back are two effective techniques. Once you have a list of courses, products, or whathaveyous, use **fax forward** to attach descriptions of these various items to the list, and to then fax both to 10 or a 1000 customers using your computer (great for efficient use of your computer while you're not in your office).

- ❑ Use **fax back** to automatically respond to someone calling for information. "If you'd like more information about Service/Product X, press 3," whereupon your Fax back program automatically retrieves the information from your computer and faxes it to the customer.

- ❑ Here're a couple of other -hints on using electronic media to stay ahead of your competition and provide great customer service.
  - You can track UPS or Fed Ex packages on your Internet. **<http://www.ups>.** (or **fedex.**) **com**
  - You can check out zip codes and other US Post Office info at **<http://www.usps.gov>**

- You can snoop around and find information about your competitors by checking them out at **<http://www.hoovers.com>**

❑ While we're on faxing: if you need to send a fax but don't have a fax or fax software but do have a computer: **<http://www-usa.tpc.int/tpc_home.html>** will convert your email to a fax and send it to your customer's fax machine **for free**!

"I've got 3 fax machines going all the time, four super fast computers and high resolution monitors, two high-speed color printers, 2 ISDN lines, fax back and fax forward programs, a voice recognition program, email, a laptop and docking system......
I do absolutely nothing myself anymore."

MiniPlans for the Technology Component of Your Business

- ❑ Review the message on your voice mail/answering machine. Better still, have someone else review it to make sure it sounds friendly, is inviting, and leaves the caller with a positive feeling and something to do. The best way to check this out is to have a potential client call, and ask them what they think. If you use a live service, make sure their service is friendly, that they answer the phone the way you want them to (not "*Can* I help you?" Of course you can. That's why they called. Try "How *may* I help you?"), and that they are prepared to handle unanticipated situations (e.g. crises). Train them, if you haven't already, and check on them frequently by calling your own number anonymously, or by having other people do so.

- ❑ To begin tracking the success of your referral/marketing network, institute a checksheet that tracks places from where your calls come. If it's a potential client, ask the caller "May I ask how you heard of me?" If it's a referral, note who it is. Use this tracking system to focus your marketing efforts.

- ❑ Thinking about computer equipment can be a daunting prospect. As soon as you buy it, equipment is out of date, so don't even think you have to keep up with it. Every soft and hardware manufacturer sets its goal to upgrade products every six months, so don't get caught up in the rat race.

  Best thing to do? If you've heard about a brand name and want to go in that direction, fine. Or if you talk with your friends and you feel comfortable following in their footsteps, that's fine too. I've been using Apple computers forever, because I initially found them friendlier. However the IBM compatibles have been trying to emulate the Apple and have, to a large extent, succeeded with the introduction of their Windows environment. So the choice should really be based on a couple of other simple things.

One, is how close the nearest dealer is who can help you solve hardware and software problems. Chances are, the programs you'll be using will be fairly simple, so you'll have no need to anticipate major software or hardware catastrophes, but you never know. And if you come to rely on your computer, as you should, you'll need someone around who can help in a pinch. Could be a vendor, a sister, brother-in-law, or good friend. Sometimes computers "crash" (just plain freeze up) for no particular reason (it happens to the best of us), so for times like that, or for times when you just plain forget how to do something, have someone around you can call on.

Two, is how much money you want to spend. Lots of people think they need the latest equipment, so they're constantly "upgrading" and getting rid of their old stuff. Don't be afraid to buy used equipment.

10% of the home-based business market buys used, and in so doing saves between 15 and 40 percent off the sticker price. Check out the Boston Computer Exchange, American Computer Exchange in Atlanta, the Dallas Magazine CompuMart, and some of the computer mail order warehouses like MacMall (1-800-552-8883), MacZone (1-800-248-0800), MacWarehouse (1-800-255-6227), MacConnection (1-800-800-2222), MacWholesale (1-800-531-4622), ClubMac (1-800-258-2622), or RTI (800-929-0029), some of which stock refurbished computers. Try to buy the computer (and printer) complete with the documentation and the manufacturer's warranty.

- ❑ Also check your dealer, the newspapers, the Classified Advertiser, or your network of friends. Just make sure the computer is new enough that it will handle the programs you want.

  For equipment, then, you need a computer (the CPU or Central Processing Unit) to do the work for you, a monitor so you can see what your computer is doing, a keyboard for typing, a mouse (and pad) for negotiating your way around the monitor screen, a printer so you can print letters and lists, and the cables to hook everything together. A little higher tech and you can get a stand-alone modem or one that's built right in to your computer so you can send email or visit the Internet.

- ❑ Computer programs are so numerous they'll drive you nutty, but a computer won't do what you want it to do unless you have the right programs for it. Because some programs are not compatible with each other, don't be surprised if your computer "crashes" or does other stupid tricks. That's why it's important to have someone you can call if things go awry and you don't know what to do or your manual proves worthless, which is usually the case.

  At a minimum, you'll need
    - ❑ A database program that you'll use to keep track of your clients and your marketing efforts.
    - ❑ A simple word processing program is also a must.
    - ❑ If you want to do a little graphic work, the better word processing programs now have limited graphic capabilities, or you can purchase a simple graphics presentations-type program.
    - ❑ A small program to keep track of any of the time you spend on any number of customers -- down to the minutes!

Technology (continued)

- ❑ A money program for invoicing. I use Blue Box Invoices for Mac (**<http://www.blueboxsw.com/>**) which uses the Filemaker program for its database. You can also get ones that balance your statements, write checks, and calculate taxes.

❑ Under the previous Office Procedures section, I discussed Contact Management Programs which are extremely useful. They are database, simple word processing and calendar programs all linked together, and can merge information into form letters, onto envelopes, and into calendars and lists.

❑ Faxing. Either get a stand-alone fax machine or a fax program for your computer (which is prone to more limitations. For example, you couldn't fax a page out of a book unless you scanned it into your computer first; and your computer has to be on 24 hours a day to receive faxes.). But for ease of use, efficiency, and speed, computer faxing can be extremely effective. (Please see discussion under electronic media for other considerations.)

"I got a few things to fax."

MiniPlans for the "Running the Business" Component of Your Business

- ❑ Make sure you have a mentor/coach who keeps you fresh, challenged, on your toes and growing as a business person.

- ❑ Set up a relationship with a marketing mentor who can help you develop your marketing plan and then keep you motivated. *Set regular office or phone appointments!* Sometimes just knowing you have an upcoming appointment will force you to complete marketing activities that won't get done otherwise.

- ❑ Most people won't mind helping you develop your business by serving on your Advisory Committee. Their sole purpose is to give you a reality check! If you tell them you really respect their judgment, and ask them to be part of a group that advises you about (your network, potential customers, your marketing materials, public relations strategies, etc.) chances are good they'll say yes.

  Naturally, the first (and subsequent) meeting needs to be efficient and well-run, but the objective is to get insight from various and varied members of the community. Your group might consist of your best referral source, a good customer, a vendor, a colleague, a lawyer, a house-husband/wife, or anyone else who has a pulse on the community. Feed them, or take them all to a private room for dinner.

- ❑ Make your billing more friendly, and make it easier for your clients to pay. Examples of friendliness:
  - handwritten notes accompanying invoices ("Thanks for your order," or "Thanks for inviting me to be part of your team," or "Great seeing you again at Rotary last week," or etc.)
  - friendly-sounding payment terms ("Unfortunately, I will need to add interest after 30 days, but you can avoid that extra charge by sending me a check or money order before the end of the month.");
  - just write "thank you" on the invoice;
  - include a special offer, or discount for their next visit/purchase.

- ❑ A survey is an excellent way for you to find out from new, existing, or previous customers how well you are doing (or did), whether they'd like to see changes in your office decor, your hours, your services, your products, how you can be more responsive, etc., etc. You can use the good things to get new clients, e.g.:
  1. If the survey concludes that people like your warm, personable style, that characteristic can be promoted in your brochure, flyer, or on your business card.
  2. If they say they like the way you help them understand their options, ask them for details and include them in your next edition of promotional materials.
  3. Use testimonials in your next brochure or on your letterhead.
  4. If the recommendation is that you change your hours of operation, change them and then put out a press release announcing the new hours and your more responsive service.

Here are some sample questions. The questionnaire can be confidential (asking for names or not), and some questions can be optional:

- **A little about yourself**: age? self-employed? entrepreneur? employee? retired? education? household income? which newspapers/magazines do you normally read?
- **About your relationship with my company**: customer for how long? where did you hear about us initially? from which of my competitors did you used to purchase? why did you choose us (saw an ad, heard about you from friend, heard you talk, etc.), which of our services/products do you purchase most often (list them)? what's the main problem you solved by coming to us? how well did we do in solving it? how would you rate the quality of our service (give them some choices)? how could we improve our service to you? Would you like us to keep in touch with you after you purchase something from us (newsletter, post card, service/product updates, phone call)? Are you aware that we are always looking for more business? would you be willing to refer us to your friends/colleagues? how do our costs compare to others?

The Business (continued)

- ❑ If you find yourself spending too much time on the details of your business — filling out paperwork, putting together mailings, tracking your contacts, billing — and not enough on marketing and working, hire a part-time "personal assistant" to help out. Many of them have computers and work from their homes (about 26 million of them), and are willing to provide just that kind of service. The cost may seem like something you can't even imagine covering right now, but you may find it pays off in the long (or possibly short) run.

"I hired a personal assistant.
She ***told*** *me to get out of the office!"*

- ❑ There are lots of financial matters to be considered. This book is not about those. Suffice it to say that if you don't have a good foundation in business principles, get it.
    - take some night or adult ed courses,
    - seek advice from the retired group of business execs (SCORE),
    - check out the government's Small Business Development (SBD) program for free consultations and references,
    - check out business departments in nearby universities or colleges for a smart intern looking for work,
    - get yourself some whizbang computer programs,
    - join a business support group (check out your Chamber), or
    - hire someone to give you advice and keep you on track.

It used to be that excellent, free advice was available from bankers, but few of them really understand the vagaries of running a business. But these days, banks aren't into taking much risk at all and tend to be overly conservative and thus not very supportive of new business ideas.

The Business (continued)

- ❑ Some advice for whether to charge an hourly rate or a fixed price for a proposed job: it all comes down to whether the customer's expectations and your ability and willingness to fulfill them are compatible. Your first task is to elicit a clear understanding of the expectations, and to then come to an understanding about what to do if there's a change in the scope of work. Most customers don't understand that what *they* might consider a small change has many ramifications that end up costing you money unless you can charge for them. This is one good reason for having a contract and a contingency fee.

  When you are first starting to set fees and figure charges, you may have to rely on "industry" averages. You can find this information on the Internet or in the library. Or if you have colleagues in the same business, you could ask them for advice. If you haven't done something before, two things need to be accounted for: (1) is that because of your "learning curve," it's going to take you substantially longer the first time than any subsequent time, and you can't charge for that "extra" time; (2) keeping accurate track of your time when you do a project. This way, you begin building a record that helps you make better estimates in the future. To help you track time, there are several small, inexpensive freeware or shareware computer programs available that track time and project names. I use one called "LogOut."

  (LogOut, Version 2.2 for MacIntosh, Copyright 1996, Jeff Miles, 5604 Stanmore Way, Elk Grove, California 95758. jeffe@aol.com.

MiniPlans for the Staying Current Component of Your Business

- ❑ Join the local Chamber of Commerce. This will keep you current about what's happening in your region. If you listen carefully (practice "active listening" techniques), you will probably pick up business trends that may help you reorient parts of your own business. Make sure you practice your 8-second pitch about your own business, and bring your cards. You are expected to exchange them.

- ❑ Read constantly. There are hundreds of new books offered every year in the business and other sections of your bookstore, or at **<http://www.amazon.com>** on the Internet. Often times I just set aside an afternoon for browsing through books and magazines. I'll find a helpful chapter here or there, or an insight or quote that will put things in perspective. Sometimes I'll even take notes. Usually I find a magazine or book so worthwhile, I'll buy it.

- ❑ Subscribe to magazines that cover business activities around the country/globe such as Inc. or Business Week (both of which are on the Internet). One magazine I've found particularly challenging and useful is *Fast Company* (no better deal around for 14 bucks a year).

- ❑ If you can, frequently browse the Internet. Use Yahoo or other search engines (I use **<http://www.ixquick.com/>**) to seek out areas of business of particular interest to you. To narrow your searches so you don't get 1000 matches, put your search words in quotes (e.g.: "wood-fired boilers", or "handmade shoes" or "communication skills training").

"Staying Current" (continued)

- ❑ Check out Internet sites oriented to small businesses such as:

  <http://www.inc.com>
  <http://www.marketingsource.com>
  <http://www.smallbiz.suny.edu/>
  <http://www.fastcompany.com/homepage/>
  <http://www.americanexpress.com/smallbusiness>
  <http://www.bizoffice.com>
  <http://smallbusiness.yahoo.com>
  <http://www.marketingsource.com>
  <http://www-sci.lib.uci.edu/HSG/RefCalculators.html>
  <http://www.hoovers.com>

- ❑ "Welcome to Small Business 2000, your weekly show on public television about the new American heroes: entrepreneurs and small business owners." Check out **<http://smallbusinessschool.org/>**

- ❑ A conversation among entrepreneurs from around the country is going on in the Running Your Business Bulletin Board; pull up a chair and join in: **<http://www.inc.com/app/discussions/>**

- ❑ Attend trade group meetings to keep current with your own industry. If you work these the right way, you'll make some good business contacts, but it can get expensive.

- ❑ Go to conferences scheduled for people who fit your profile of potential customers; check out **<http://www.TSNN.com>** for upcoming conferences. Conference-going can be expensive.

- ❑ Join one or more **leads groups** where members talk about their businesses, share information about possible

"Staying Current" (continued)

customers, and pass on leads.

- ❑ Some people find time to watch business, technology, and science programs on TV which cover research and/or breaking news in their areas of interest.

- ❑ You may wish to subscribe to trade journals or newsletters which can be excellent sources of information. Browse the Internet for consultant and corporate newsletters (some are free). Most professional and business associations now have their own websites where material is often cross-referenced (linked) to other websites of a similar nature, and where newsletters are available.

Other Online Info Sources

1-800-MYLOGO <http://www.1800mylogo.com/> Professional logos, slogans and jingles for small and medium sized businesses at great prices. Nice website with plenty of excellent design samples to view.

4over Inc. <http://www.4over.com/> One of the many on-line printing services.

Americanexpress.com <http://www.americanexpress.com/homepage/smallbusiness.shtml?> Under the "Managing Your Business section, "Business Resources,"
check out: Learn from online business resources, Use interactive business tools, Benefit from expert advice.

American Telecommuting Association <http://www.knowledgetree.com/ata.html> Information for telecommuters. Free publication "How Can I Start Telecommuting?"

Bplans.com <http://Bplans.com/> The small business planning resource center. Free sample plans. Software support and information. Bplans.com supports the process of writing a business plan.

Business@Home <http://www.gohome.com/index.html> Online version of print magazine devoted to working at home. The articles have a different take on small business with a clean, crisp, and organized layout.

Business Plan Store <http://www.netaxs.com/~bps/> The Business Plan Store writes affordable, confidential business plans.

Business Resource Center <http://www.morebusiness.com/> a business resource center with tools, templates, articles, etc.

Calculators On-Line Center http://www.americanexpress.com/homepage/smallbusiness.shtml? This is a phenomenal site! It contains over 10,260 Calculators created by over 2,040 very CREATIVE Individuals.

DECA <http://www.deca.org/> An association of high school and college marketing students. Links, scholarships, contests.

E Library <http://ask.elibrary.com/> "Research without legwork" Great site! Research access to major newpapers, magazines, transcripts, pictures, maps, and books. 7 day free service with monthly and yearly services available.

Entrepreneurial Edge <http://edge.lowe.org> "Over 1,415 ideas to help you Grow Your Company"

"Staying Current" (continued)

Entrepreneur Magazine <http://www.entrepreneurmag.com/> On-line edition of Entrepreneur magazine. Includes search through prior 5 years of articles, small business shareware library, bulletin board, chat rooms, and more.

Fast Company <http://www.fastcompany.com/homepage/> Lots of exciting articles about emerging businesses. The site is well organized and covers up to date issues for today's entrepreneur.

IdeaCafe <http://www.ideacafe.com/> "Small Business Grant Center" Information about financing your business from a variety of sources. Preparing for financing. Capital raising insights. Fun, well organized layout.

Inc. Magazine Online <http://www.inc.com/> Great site for entrepreneurs - articles, tips. Interact with others. Build a website online.

Law Research <http://www.lawresearch.com> Search legal opinions and legislation across the USA for free.

Management Library <http://www.managementlibrary.com/> "A leading research database of best-practice management strategies. Library is comprised of proprietary information from the Institute of Management and Administration's 58+ specialized business publications, and contains nearly 9,000 articles for niche business applications. Library includes survey data, case studies, analyses, and, best of all, practical, how-to advice not found anywhere else."

National Association for the Self Employed <http://www.nase.org/> Offers benefits and services previously available only to large corporations.

Newspapers.com <http://www.newspapers.com> Links to newspapers all over the world.

On-Line Small Business Workshop <http://www.sb.gov.bc.ca/smallbus/workshop/workshop.html> Step-by-step advice on building a business. Presented by the British Columbia Provincial Government.

PR Web "The Free Wire Service" <http://www.prweb.com/login.php> Free press release submission service.

Radio Programs and Personalities <http://www.radiospace.com/programs.htm> Has hundreds of links to Radio Computer and Technology Shows, Syndicated Talk Shows and Personalities, Nationally Distributed Public-Radio Shows, Other Nationally Syndicated Offerings, and Popular Local Personalities and Shows.

SBA Homepage <http://www.sba.gov/> Information on starting a business, SBA loans, and other helpful services for business owners

Silicon Valley Small Business Development Center <http://www.siliconvalley-sbdc.org/busplan.html> The Small Business Center helps with growing a business. Sponsored by the SBA.

Small Business Advancement National Center <http://www.sbaer.uca.edu/> "Small business counseling and electronic resource information center." Award winning small business site containing one of the world's largest online information-bases. Info includes: Industry Profiles, International Business, Family Business, Business Planning, Demographics, and Contact Databases.

Small Business Information Guide for The Mining Company <http://sbinformation.miningco.com/> Information for small business owners and entrepreneurs. Weekly features, guest experts, tips and tools, annotated links, chat boards, a newsletter, top business books and more. Excellent links!

Small Office Home Office <http://www.soho.org/> "SOHO Online can help you manage the challenges of working in a small office/home office environment.>

The Right Site® <http://www.easidemographics.com/> Demographic reference and site selection service.

The Small Business Advisor <http://www.isquare.com/> A wide variety of information for the entrepreneur and small business owner. Daily business news and marketing tips with full site search capability.

Trade Show News Network <http://www2.tsnn.com/> Lists worldwide trade shows and conferences. A comprehensive listing helping you find Tradeshows, Exhibitors, Suppliers. If you work these the right way, you'll make some good business contacts, but it can get expensive.

Part 4

The Complete Marketing Plan

Way, way back I introduced the idea of breaking your marketing into two activities: marketing your business and marketing your product/service. They're interrelated, for sure, but the idea was to make sure you were aware that the way in which you "run" your business plays a critical role in your success. Another reason to break apart marketing activities is because marketing your business involves activities that are pretty generic.

Marketing your services/products, on the other hand, involves activities that are very, very specific.

As an example, you wouldn't market a car the same way you'd market a computer or wedding ring. You wouldn't market a computer repair service the same way you'd market an auto repair service, or a dental service the same way you'd market a therapy service. There's a good chance you're not going to market men's shoes the same way you'd market women's shoes. And so on.

Each of these requires a careful look at a whole range of very specific considerations.

What follows is a comprehensive outline with explanations. It's designed to help you discover aspects of marketing you probably never knew existed. It's the kind of outline used when doing market research. Much of it can be filled in by using your "gut" instincts because, after all, you probably know your customer base pretty well.

The premise is that there's gold in the details, and if you dig enough, and roll it around enough, good stuff will fall out.

Even if you complete only bits and pieces, you'll be better off. And you can keep refining and redoing parts as you learn more throughout the next few months.

Note:

At the end of Part 4 is a blank outline of the Marketing Plan for Products and Services. I've even removed the book's page numbers.

Depending on your needs, you could just fill in the outline by hand, "type" it in with one of those old fashioned machines, or redo it on your word processor. This latter may seem a little cumbersome, but it'll give you time to think about what you're writing.

If you think it would be easier, for $5 (including shipping) I'm also happy to send you a 3.5" disk with the Marketing Plan outline saved to an ASCI file so you can open it on either a Mac or IBM system.

Just call me at **1-888-290-8405**.

The Complete Marketing Plan

A. Target Markets

1. What characteristics distinguish your primary "target market?"

A "target market" is the potential customer you're zeroing in on. Though you may be able to identify several, please list the one customer who/which would be your *primary* target. A potential customer may either be described as an individual needing service/products (e.g. an owner of a small business) or as a group (e.g. dentists). Be careful in your selection, as efforts to penetrate target markets that are too broad are usually ineffective. Answer these questions:

a. **Critical needs**: for the kind of customer you'd like to service, what are their most critical needs that you'll be able to fulfill? For example, if the target you've identified is "owners of small businesses," exactly what are their critical needs?

b. **To what degree are those needs now being met**? Are your prospective customer's needs something that can be fulfilled by any other business? (The fewer ways their needs can be satisfied, the higher the likelihood that you could become their vendor, therapist, mechanic, marketing consultant, REALTOR®.) To the extent that you can:

   1. List the ways in which you think the needs of the potential customer are now being met. List the names of other businesses, consultants, products, free services.

   2. Comment on the extent to which you think these service/products are being met within your catchment area. Use a "gut level" percentage figure if you don't have statistics.

c. **Demographics**:
   Each prospect has (its) own demographics. For example: for individuals they might be age range, gender, income range, financial health, ability to pay, educational achievement, place of residence, marital status, family status, occupation, health priorities. For groups, for example:

Notes

Notes

age of organizations, number of employees, average age of employees, cash flow status, management structure, seasonal affects, staff capabilities, level of productivity. Please be as specific as possible. Use the following list to begin profiling your *existing* customer. This will help you get a handle on the kind of *new* prospects you might try reaching.

d. **Geographic location**. If you know the distance your current customers are willing to travel for your services/products, there's a good chance new ones will be willing to travel that distance as well. Further, as many of your new customers may be referrals from existing customers, it makes sense to market your service/products in the same areas.

e. **Who makes the decision to purchase your services/products?** You can break this question into several parts depending on whether you're going after individuals, organizations, or both. The idea is to find out who makes the final decision to commit money, and to then find ways to influence that decision. This is an attempt to find out who actually makes the decisions to spend the money where more than one individual/group is involved. For instance, if one of your prospects is the CEO, do they make the decision to purchase services/products? If one of your targets is IBM, which corporate individual or committee actually makes the decision to use a particular service/product provider?

f. **Seasonal/cyclical/causal trends**. Sometimes customers seem to come in bunches. You may be able to trace the reason for that bunching. Did school just start, or a competitor just move out of the area? Did another consultant/company drop--or add-- a service/product which results in enhancing the options of potential customers coming to you? Does a major employer always give out raises at the same time of year? If you can identify these situations, you might be able to influence them or, more likely, take advantage of them by putting your business out in front of them.

2. Primary target market size

a. **Number of prospective customers**. Trying to identify this gives you hope (or it could discourage you and force you to change direction). Basically, if you've identified the kinds of customers you'd like to have, and you can fairly clearly identify where they come from, you might be able to get a handle on how many might be in that group. If the group you identify is,

Notes

for instance, all CEOs between the ages of 25 and 45 who own companies with 100 or more employees, the base group upon which you can draw is enormous. If, however, your targeted market is the adolescent buyer between the ages of 13 and 15, living in a single parent household, your base group might be very small. Your prospects for new customers from the former group are certainly much higher than they would be from the latter group. So — what do you think is the size of your prospective group?

b. **Annual purchase of service/products meeting the same or similar needs as your service/ products**. Again, this is here to give you hope. If, for instance, you know that the public is spending $100 billion per year on home decorating services/products, and that the amount spent is growing by 15% per year, your home decorating consulting services are in the right market and have a good chance of making it. So — can you find out what this figure is for your business?

c. **Anticipated market growth**. Same reasoning here. What's the industry saying? The answer, by the way, may give you insights about ways in which you need to change your business to reflect changing times.

3. Market penetration - Indicate the extent to which you anticipate penetrating your market and demonstrate why you feel that level of penetration is achievable based on your market research.

a. **Market share**. Talk a bit here about what you consider might be your percentage of the market share. You may not come up with a specific figure, but it does give you reason to think about competition. If you do begin developing harder numbers (which I'd encourage), you can use them to set a goal for your business and to then measure the impact of your marketing efforts.

b. **Number of customers**. Again, use your best judgment to set a target goal for your business. Three things need to come together here: The number of purchases, the amount you charge per service/product, and the income you need to pay your bills, enjoy yourself, and get ready for retirement. Given that equation, how many customers do you need?

c. **Geographic coverage**. How far can you realistically extend your service/distribution area?

d. **Rationale for market penetration estimates**. As you might do in working the figure for a proposal, or for your taxes at the end of the year, develop a worksheet of notes that show how you arrived at the above information. This gives you a benchmark for evaluating your reasoning and your progress at the end of the year.

4. Pricing

a. **Price levels**. Keep your pricing structure within range of the industry standards in your area of the country. If you're not getting customers, lowering your price is not going to bring them to your door. Raising the value of your service/products just may.

b. **Discount structure (volume, prompt payment, etc.)**. Whether this kind of reasoning makes any sense for your business is up to you to determine. If you're providing a lot of services/products to one customer, you may want to offer a discounting structure that makes them feel like you're making a concession to their loyalty and their level of business with you.

5. Methods by which specific members of your target market can be identified. This is my favorite area, because it's the first time a certain kind of reality has to be faced. All the above research was an attempt to qualify and quantify your search for the perfect customers. Now you need to figure out exactly how you're going to find them. Be really creative. This is like panning for gold. (See previous sections in this book for help here.) Would you look to use:

a. **Directories**? Which ones?

b. **Trade association publications**? Which ones?

c. **List Brokers**? What would you ask them to sort for?

d. **New referral sources?** Who? Which ones?

e. **Corporate newsletters?** Which ones? How will you get them?

f. **Is there any other way you might reach potential customers?**

Notes

Notes

6. Media through which you can communicate with specific members of your target market. Now that you've identified the potential customers and how you might be able to find them, you need to figure out how you're going to reach them! Would you reach potential customers through:

a. **Publications**? Would you advertise (be cautious!)? Write articles? Report on certain events? What would you do?

b. **Radio/television broadcasts**? Become a talk show host? Call in frequently to other talk shows? Market yourself as the expert that editors seek out for information?

c. **Sources of influence and/or advice**? If you know most of your potential customers will probably be referred by family physicians, for example, those physicians would be people of influence through whom you can affect decisions made by your potential customers! From whom else would the majority of your potential customers seek opinion, information, ideas, recommendations? What other sources of influence might you be able to affect in some fashion?

7. Decision-Making process. This is a real neat area to think through. No one makes a decision to spend money without thought. The decision-making process through which a person must go before deciding to buy from you is probably fairly predictable, and would probably progress through the following schedule. Comment on each by indicating ways in which you might be able to influence the process.

a. **Needs identification**: What will help your potential customers identify the fact that they may have a need for the kind of services/products you provide? How can you help them identify those needs? Don't be circuitous here. Draw obvious connections that your potential customers might make given their reference frameworks.

b. **Research for solution to needs:** In their search for ways to satisfy their needs, will your potential customers run across your name/the name of your business and the benefits they'll get by working with you? Will they see a list of the ways you might be able to help them? Will they be encouraged to call you and you alone? What could you do to influence this part of their process?

c. **Solution evaluation process:** When your potential customers start assimilating and sorting through the information they've gathered, how will you make sure they keep your name/business in the forefront, ahead of all your competitors? What can you do in the relationship-building process that fixes you in their minds to the point where they will always drift toward your phone number?

d. **Final solution selection:** and decision to call and make an appointment/purchase.

8. Key trends and anticipated changes within your primary target markets. I encourage you to think about this only so you don't get caught behind the eight ball. If you see even the slightest changes taking place, you need to get out in front of them and figure out how your business should change to stay current. Maybe it's just a matter of keeping your customers informed. Maybe it's offering new services/products during a crisis (fresh water during a flood, home building services after a hurricane).

B. Market Test Results

This is also a fascinating area of marketing research. If you speak with customers, and you decide to offer another service/product based on their advice, you should check out the offering before making it really public. Years ago, one of the reasons I opened a gourmet food store is because several of my friends told me they'd be there all the time! Luckily, the store had a lot of other things going for it, because I never did see those people very much. There's nothing like the test of the market itself. Try developing a prototype of the service/product you want to offer. Go into it slowly. Try some of the following:

1. Contact potential referral sources. First, figure out who they would be. Then you need to figure out a way to approach them that is comfortable for you and that ensures their receptivity. Share your idea with them, and ask for their feedback. You will probably not actually sell it to them, but just by telling them about it, two things are accomplished: they now know you have the service/product, and they feel like you really value

Notes

their input, which builds trust between you (the first step in creating a relationship).

2. Give potential customers information and/or demonstrations. This is the best way to find out whether what *you* think people need/want is what *they* think they need/want. It also gives you the opportunity to say "This is a test run," in case there are obvious changes that must be made. Again, the more you do with this phase of testing, the more potential customers you impact, and the more the word gets out without you actually "selling" yourself.

3. Reaction of potential customers. Measure and evaluate their reaction. You might need to change the services/product, then try it out again. The more your test customers see you and see your willingness to "get it right," the better they feel about the way in which you might be able to help them (now or at some later date).

4. Test Group's willingness to purchase services/ products at your price level. Just what it says. Is there a breaking point beyond which they can't justify spending the money? Probably, but you may never be able to get a handle on it. Keep in mind that if people really *want* something (not *need*, but *want* something), there's a good chance they'll find some way to get it. Think of all the purchases you or your business have made, even when the day before you said you had no money? Somehow, you made it happen because you wanted that service/product more than anything in the world. People do that, and, in your case, if by emphasizing the benefits of your products/services you can help them put their need into the "want" category, you will be at an advantage.

C. Lead Times (Here's the technical jargon: Amount of time between customer order placement and service/product delivery). If one of your good referral sources suggests that you develop a needed service/product, how long does it take you to develop, test, and offer it? The answer to this question keeps you from making promises you can't keep, but also helps you sound professional when someone asks you to consider offering something new.

Other areas to be investigated include the time it takes you to follow up on leads for prospective customers, processing requests for appointments, scheduling call backs, obtaining information, or checking credit.

Notes

Notes

The best way to handle this section might be to chronicle the history of four random but typical customer accounts and compare them to a time schedule you think is reasonable, or one that you know will make your customers happy. Also make notes about areas in which you think your processing times could be (or have been) reduced because of specially developed procedures, or etc. You may discover marketable ideas that could add unique value for prospective customers.

D. Competition

This is probably one of the more important items on this outline. How you view, think about, and react to competition will have a major impact on the way you do business and how much of it you do.

First of all, you need to *know* the competition — for many reasons. Get out there and find out who's offering what kinds of services/products. What do they charge for them? What kinds of value do they add to them? What kind of customer services are they providing? What are they doing differently from you? If you have no immediate competition right around you, go to some lengths to find out what other businesses are offering anyway. The reasons? First of all, you don't want to get the reputation of being outdated, not up with the times. If other offices are sending out follow-up letters after a sale, and they're doing it because studies have proved that customers like the contact, you should know that, and perhaps replicate the idea.

Secondly, by having your finger on the pulse of the business, you can stay ahead of new ideas. It's embarrassing when a customer reads in Time Magazine about some new office product that cuts paper costs in half, and then asks you, the office organizer consultant, about it — especially when you haven't read Time Magazine! Naturally, you can't know everything, but keeping your information feelers out will keep you excited and connected and, most importantly, will help you become "the expert."

Being an "expert" is good, because then people accord you a certain status that keeps you in mind. If there's a public referendum, for instance, "officials" might call you, or the news media thinks you might help them help the public understand what's going on. And that keeps your name in front of people. Thirdly, knowing the kind of work your competitors do will help you "find your niche" or "position"* your business. A slight variation on a theme, or adding just a touch of difference to the way things are normally done, might affect whether you get the next customer.

* The key to successful positioning is threefold:

1. Determine the customer type attracted by the business's identity;
2. Understand what they consider important;
3. Find and stress ways in which the business fills those important needs.

Benchmarking

The term "benchmarking" today refers to an organization's desire to improve by emulating another company cited for "best business" in the particular area in which improvement is sought. Though multinational companies are benchmarking regularly, smaller organizations are generally too concerned with protecting their own customer base to share information with potential competitors.

Nevertheless, I feel there may be opportunities to adapt the benchmarking concept in an environment where smaller groups feel secure enough to share information and, perhaps, even to work together -- collaborate -- in some areas.

It would be helpful if you brainstormed with yourself, your staff, and/or your business peers about areas in which collaboration could occur with facilities, service/products, training, equipment, advertising, marketing, networking, purchasing, and support services/products.

At the least, we may uncover other potential sources of revenue.

With all that in mind, who is your competition?

1. List existing competition

Evaluating competition is somewhat tricky in that the variables are numerous and not always comparable. Depending on the importance you give this section, you can be as detailed or as global as necessary in evaluating and developing your special niche(s).

Following are the kinds of criteria that could be used for comparisons:

Notes

Notes

- number of employees
- variety of services/products
- depth or services/products
- gross income
- number in customer base
- square footage of office
- parking availability
- hours of operation
- marketing program
- product enhancements (values added)
- customer service policy
- cost of similar products/services
- follow-up policy

a. Direct competition:

Try preparing a list of those businesses which are *exactly* like yours in the above areas and which are within the geographic reach of your business.

Then try preparing a list of those businesses which you feel are *similar* to yours which are within the geographic reach of your business.

Are there any businesses you feel are similar to yours that are *outside* your geographic reach, but which are encroaching on your business?

b. Indirect Competition:

Indirect competition is any activity or process which gives your customers (or potential customers) the option to spend money they would otherwise spend buying services/products from you. Indirect competition is effective when it convinces your customers (or potential customers) to lower the priority for your services/ products and raise the priority for theirs.

When seen in this light, indirect competition could be new tires for the car, a vacation weekend, self-help books, audio/video training programs, imminent downsizing, home-made tarragon vinegar, or the need for a new computer networking system (if you market to big corporations).

To the best of your ability, and probably based on unrecorded conversations with your customers or at a Chamber meeting, what would you say would be your list of indirect competitors? Would you be able to list them (or number them) in priority order?

Notes

c. Determine competition's market share

While in the process of listing your competitors, try determining what share of the market you think they have. We're more interested in your guestimate, regardless of whether the numbers add up to 100%, because this will also tell us what you perceive their impact to be. As an example, it's OK if you think competitor X is grabbing "a good 70% of the market share" and that indirect competitor Y corners 65% and that competitor Z is probably taking 5%.

This tells us that X and Y need to be reckoned with in some fashion, but that Z is probably having little or no effect on your actual or perceived customer base.

d. Potential How long will your "window of opportunity" be open before your success breeds new competition that erodes your business? Who will your new competitors likely be?

Success breeds competition, so the better you do, the more competition you'll have. If you're making money, and doing a good job at it, your competitors will want to know why and how, and they'll want a piece of the action. Keep in mind, however, that more competition also means that the public is becoming more sophisticated -- which is *great* for *all* your businesses!

You can set yourself apart while keeping your business vibrant if you provide *better* products, *better* services and *better* values, so that you maintain or build your market share.

2. Strengths or competitive advantages

A careful self-analysis of your business will pinpoint internal organizational, technological, or personal areas that can be categorized as "best business practices" and that set you apart from other providers. This is not a place to be bashful or modest. Try convincing your potential customers that you *are* the best and *have* the best!

These statements can be very helpful in a number of ways. First, if you decide to prepare any marketing

Notes

materials, you have ready-made information. Second, the more clear you are about who you are and what you do, the easier it is to convince other people that you know what you're doing and that you're the best. Third, is the matter of feeling good. It's all too easy to be critical; it's much harder to pat yourself on the back. If you can learn how to talk to yourself in the third person, and to use that approach to praise yourself for the good work you do or products you provide, you'll *feel* good. The better you feel, the more positively you can talk about your business in a way that makes people feel good about it and you.

a. Ability to satisfy customer needs.
Try answering this as *subjectively* as possible. We want to know what your customers say about this, how they react to your attempts to satisfy their needs — and how you've been going about it. Are you doing anything special? What makes you more able than another provider? This can be turned into a competitive advantage.

b. Market penetration
The fact that your business is still healthy and has the potential to grow means that you have already penetrated one or more of your markets. If you can, describe how you're feeling about your accomplishments to date, and whether you can think of fresh ways to make more inroads.

c. Track record and reputation
Talk about the reputation you have among your customers, your peers and the general public. Break it into those three areas and try to be as accurate and as complete as possible. You can build on this in innumerable ways. The more credibility you have, the faster you can build your image.

d. Staying power; financial resources
You've already proved you have staying power. But take a minute to spell out a little more clearly how you're putting money back into the business, investing in training, or upgrading the office and equipment.

e. Key personnel
Write a short bio about yourself, emphasizing not only your educational and training credentials, but also your attitude toward your business and your customers. Describe something about the way you arrived at your philosophy, your background, and

Notes

what makes you particularly suited to do what you do, and what kinds of business experiences or growth opportunities you've had to date. Do the same for the rest of your staff. It's also important that you include on your list all the people you rely on for outside business assistance (lawyer, banker, accountant, marketing consultant, graphics designer, printer). The idea is to account for everyone on your team so you and others know you have your bases covered.

3. Competitive disadvantages

Note that the subtitles in this section reads exactly the same as in the previous section. However, this section is here to help you look carefully at your competitive disadvantages- *real or perceived* - that may affect your business. If anyone could bring themselves to say negative things about you or your business, what might they say? Be as objective as you can possibly be!

a. Ability to satisfy customer needs

Do you have the ability to satisfy your customers' needs? If you're thinking no one is asking for other services/products and that therefore they don't need them, make sure it's not a case of them not asking because you're not offering.

b. Market penetration

c. Track record and reputation

d. Staying power; financial resources

e. Key personnel

Everyone has limitations. The key is to make sure those limitations don't adversely affect your business. You can do this by making sure the right people are aligned with the right responsibilities. If you're lacking expertise in a certain area, buy it elsewhere.

You should also be sensitive to factors that might be negatively influencing you and your staff, such as the tendency to avoid success. It's a common phenomenon which is manifested in various ways. As an example, you may avoid responding to an invitation to present a paper at a conference because you "can't find the time." Instead, says success-avoidance expert Gerri King, Ph.D., it may be that you want to avoid the notoriety so you won't be invited to speak at other conferences, or you may feel like an imposter because you're convinced that others will do a better job.

These are all ways of "avoiding success" and are barriers to being able to do things that make businesses successful.

4. Importance of your target market to others in business.

You may be after some of the same markets as your competitors. However, if you establish a niche business, you may have no competition. In the long run, an extremely successful business will naturally invite competition. To establish and hang on to market dominance, you need to effect and maintain sound marketing strategies.

Try determining whether your potential competitors are *really* interested in your targeted markets.

5. Barriers to entry into the market

Take this opportunity to look at the following list and accurately detail what might prevent you from expanding into new market territories.

a. Cost (investment)
b. Time
c. Technology
d. Key personnel
e. Customer inertia (loyalty to another business, existing relationships, or lack of education)

Notes

Marketing Plan Outline

The following pages comprise a blank outline of the previous several pages. If you come across phrases you don't understand, just go back to the previous section and read the explanation.

You're welcome to copy these pages and use them as is, or to retype them as you go. Or, for $4.95, I'd be glad to send you a disk with the outline formatted in ASCI text so you can open and use it in your own word processing program. Order online at

<http://www.minimarketing.com>

or from

Ron King Associates
85 Warren Street, Concord, NH 03301
888-290-8405
email ron@minimarketing.com)

Marketing Plan
for Products & Services

A Plan

to Provide Information
for Marketing

____

name of product/service

to

____

prospective customer

By ______________________________

your name

Date: ____________________

Marketing Plan
for Products & Services

A. Target Markets

1. What characteristics distinguish your primary "target market?"

a. **Critical needs**:

b. **To what degree are those needs now being met**.

1 List the ways in which you think the needs of the potential customer are now being met. List the names of other businesses, consultants, products, free services.

2 Comment on the extent to which you think these service/products are being met within your catchment area. Use a "gut level" percentage figure if you don't have statistics.

c. **Demographics** My ideal customer is/has:

d. **Geographic location**.

e. **Who makes the decision to purchase your services/products?**

f. **Seasonal/cyclical trends**.

2. Primary target market size

   a. **Number of prospective customers**.

   b. **Annual purchase of service/products meeting the same or similar needs as your service/products**.

   c. **Anticipated market growth**.

3. Market penetration

   a. **Market share**.

   b. **Number of customers**. Again, use your best judgment to set a target goal for your business.

   c. **Geographic coverage**.

   d. **Rationale for market penetration estimates**.

4. Pricing

   a. **Price levels**.

   b. **Discount structure (for volume purchases, prompt payment, long-term commitments)**.

5. Methods by which specific members of your target market can be identified.

   a. **Directories**? Which ones?

   b. **Trade association publications**? Which ones?

   c. **List Brokers**? What would you ask them to sort for?

   d. **New referral sources?** Who? Which ones?

   e. **Corporate newsletters?** Which ones? How will you get them?

f. **Is there any other way you might reach potential customers?**

6. Media through which you can communicate with specific members of your target market.

a. **Publications**?

b. **Radio/television broadcasts**?

c. **Sources of influence and/or advice**?

7. Decision-Making process.

a. **Needs identification**:

b. **Research for solution to needs**

c. **Solution evaluation process**

d. **Final solution selection**

8. Key trends and anticipated changes within your primary target markets.

B. Market Test Results

1. Contact potential referral sources.

2. Give potential customers information and/or demonstrations.

3. Reaction of potential customers.

4. Test Group's willingness to purchase services/products at your price level.

C. Lead Times

D. Competition

1. List existing competition

   a. Direct competition:

   b. Indirect Competition:

   c. Determine the competition's market share

   d. Potential

2. Strengths (competitive advantages)

   a. Ability to satisfy customer needs.

   b. Market penetration

c. Track record and reputation

d. Staying power (financial resources)

e. Key personnel

3. Competitive disadvantages

a. Ability to satisfy customer needs

b. Market penetration

c. Track record and reputation

d. Staying power (financial resources)

e. Key personnel

4. Importance of your target market to others in business.

5. Barriers to entry into the market

a. Cost (investment)

b. Time

c. Technology

d. Key personnel

e. Customer inertia (loyalty to another business, existing relationships, lack of education, etc.)

Part 5

What To Do Next

What To Do Next

The reason I gave you an "Introduction to Marketing," talked about "The Marketing Process," and suggested you complete the many exercises in this book was so you'd develop a "*sixth sense*" about marketing. A lot of marketing decisions you'll make will be in response to a particular situation that'll require a reaction, right there on the spot. An opportunity, say, that you hadn't anticipated. So the more familiar you are with the concepts behind marketing, the better your "gut instincts" will be.

"What To Do Next" is always a question when you finish a book of this nature, because you have so much information, you just don't know where to start. But now you need to use what you've learned, so here's what you do:

1. Figure out whether you need a marketing plan.

2. If yes, decide whether you want to market your product/service or one component of your business

3. If it's a p/s,

- **Decide to whom you want to market (your target market),**
- **Make sure your p/s satisfies one of their needs.**
- **Develop a strategy for contacting your target market.**
- **Set up a contact management plan.**
- **Commit to a start and end time.**
- **Commit to the dollars needed (if any).**
- **Implement the plan!**

4. If it's one component of your business:

- **Decide which one(s).**
- **Decide what you want to do about /with it.**
- **Develop a strategy for doing it.**
- **Commit to a start and end time.**
- **Commit to the dollars needed (if any).**
- **Implement the plan!**

Congratulations!

You're done! Now -- do yourself and your business a **huge** favor and keep up the good work!

Please let me know if I may help you in any way.

Ron King

ron@minimarketing.com

Beckwith, Harry, *Selling the Invisible*, Warner Books, 1997.

Conner, Richard, and Jeffrey Davidson, *Marketing Your Consulting and Professional Services*, John Wiley and Sons, New York, 1985.

Crandall, Rick, *Marketing Your Services: for people who hate to sell*, Select Press, California, 1995.

Davidson, Jeff, *Marketing on a Shoestring*, John Wiley & Sons, New York, 1994.

Gumpert, D.E., *How to Really Create a Successful Marketing Plan*, Inc. Magazine, Revised and updated, 1994.

Levinson, Jay Conrad, *Guerrilla Marketing: Secrets for making big profits from your small business*; Houghton Mifflin, New York, 1993.

Misner, Ivan, *The World's Best Known Marketing Secrets: Building Your Business With Word-Of-Mouth Marketing*, Bard and Stephen, 1994.

Nash, Edward, *Database Marketing: the Ultimate Marketing Tool*, McGraw Hill, New York, 1992.

Peters, Tom, *Crazy Times Call for Crazy Organizations*, Vintage Books, 1994.

Rapp, Stan, and Thomas Collins, *The New Maximarketing*, McGraw Hill, New York, 1995.

Ries, Al, and Jack Trout, *The 22 Immutable Laws of Marketing*, Harper Business, New York, 1993.

Slutsky, Jeff, *How to Get Clients*; Warner Books, New York, 1992.

Wilson, Jerry R., *Word-of-Mouth Marketing*, John Wiley & Sons, New York, 1994.

About Ron King

Ron King, a graduate of Cornell University and the University of Pennsylvania Graduate School of Architecture, is an entrepreneur's entrepreneur who has founded more than 7 successful enterprises. His architecture, design, business, and marketing backgrounds give him a unique perspective that continues to bring benefits to his varied clientele year after year.

His low-cost, no-cost approach to marketing is welcomed by owners of small to medium-sized businesses, entrepreneurs, and individuals in private practice exhibiting a success-oriented attitude and a desire to make their marketing approach work NOW.

Ron King Associates is a customer-driven marketing firm also providing design, writing, editing, and desk-top publishing services, and hands-on marketing workshops for owners of small businesses.

Please Note

We are always looking for ways to improve this book. If you have suggestions, please call, email, fax, or send us the completed form at the end of the book.

Ron King

85 Warren St, Concord NH 03301
email: ron@minimarketing.com
phone: 603•228•0476
fax: 603-228-6018
Phone Outside NH 888-290-8405

Mini Marketing

Pelican Publishing Company
1000 Burmaster Street, Gretna, La. 70053

Send me ____________ copies at $19.95 each (plus $2.25 postage and handling for first copy and 60 cents each thereafter). Louisiana residents include sales tax.

Enclosed is my check or money order for ________________________________

Name ____

Address ____

Mini Marketing

Pelican Publishing Company
1000 Burmaster Street, Gretna, La. 70053

Send me ____________ copies at $19.95 each (plus $2.25 postage and handling for first copy and 60 cents each thereafter). Louisiana residents include sales tax.

Enclosed is my check or money order for ________________________________

Name ____

Address ____

Mini Marketing

Pelican Publishing Company
1000 Burmaster Street, Gretna, La. 70053

Send me ____________ copies at $19.95 each (plus $2.25 postage and handling for first copy and 60 cents each thereafter). Louisiana residents include sales tax.

Enclosed is my check or money order for ________________________________

Name ____

Address ____

Index